D0921562

"Practical and with a clear sense of purpose, *Backstory Preaching* encourages preachers to embrace and embody their own story of God as a critical component of biblical interpretation and sermon preparation. Cressman invites a rather elusive yet much needed commodity among preachers—the integration of life, spirituality, and the craft of preaching. The result of working through this book will be a preacher with a renewed sense of call—and the skills to carry it out."

> —Rev. Karoline M. Lewis
> Marbury E. Anderson Chair in Biblical Preaching

"Lisa Cressman has given us a warmly human, practical, yet deeply spiritual and refreshing reflection on the vocation of the preacher—a gift of prayer for us, really. She reminds us of the heart of the matter: the experience of God's passionate love. Preachers, do yourself a favor: get this book and take it on retreat. It will warm your soul—and therein lies the key to better preaching."

> —Rev. Michael E. Connors, CSC, Director
> The John S. Marten Program in Homiletics and Liturgics
> University of Notre Dame

"Preachers who pick up this book will sit down for a wide-ranging, free-wheeling, vividly focused conversation with a colleague—one who *knows* firsthand, and who *names* succinctly not just the 'in's and out's,' but the 'up's and down's' of the vocation you share. With art and energy, Lisa Cressman has written not a *textbook* for preaching, but a *spirituality* of preaching—one pervaded with compassionate wisdom and practical strategies for soul formation, sermon formation, and the disciplined practices of heart and mind that bring both together in a lifegiving process of mutually creative nurture. Unequivocal about the demands of the vocation and the disciplines it requires, she demonstrates, with humor and insight, how the duties of preaching can become sources of personal delight."

> —David J. Schlafer, author of *Your Way with God's Word,*
> and *Playing with Fire: Preaching Work as Kindling Art*

"For every preacher who has wished for a trusted colleague with whom to share wisdom and insight about the craft of preaching, Lisa Cressman is a true find. An accomplished preacher herself, she writes candidly, conversationally, and compassionately—preacher-to-preacher, friend-to-friend—about both the stress and joy of crafting sermons. There is much valuable and practical advice to be gleaned in this volume, but the main virtue of this book is Cressman's compelling vision of the preaching task, so deeply rooted in prayer and so firmly focused on the gospel."

—Thomas G. Long
Bandy Professor Emeritus of Preaching
Candler School of Theology, Emory University

"Long ago, Aristotle said that one of the three key ingredients in an effective communication situation is *ethos,* the listener's perception of the character of the speaker. Lisa Cressman goes significantly farther by emphasizing that the character, the person, of the preacher is formative for preachers themselves. We do not prepare to preach just by engaging in biblical interpretation, reflecting theologically, and relating hermeneutically to the congregation. We prepare for preaching by becoming people whose life is shaped by the gospel so that preaching is an authentic expression of who we are. The sermon embodies the person of the preacher. The book helps us preachers become aware in a critical way of the backstories that are at work in us and that inevitably contribute to our preaching, and she shows us how to deepen and broaden those stories through the practice of *lectio divina*. This volume will be a great read for the individual preacher, a wonderful resource for clergy colleague groups, and an excellent addition to preaching classes in lay preacher training, Bible colleges, and seminaries."

—Ronald J. Allen
Professor of Preaching, and Gospels and Letters
Christian Theological Seminary

"*Backstory Preaching* brings sermon formation and spiritual formation into a richly textured conversation. Cressman argues that life-giving sermons emerge within relationships of deep trust, shaped by spiritual authenticity and truth-telling. Reading this book and taking the suggested practices to heart will not only improve your preaching, but may also change your preaching ministry into a life-long spiritual journey."

—John S. McClure
Charles G. Finney Professor of Preaching and Worship
Vanderbilt Divinity School

"It is true that clergy who have worked with The Rev. Lisa Cressman and have practiced the Backstory Preaching method are better preachers for having done so. However, this is no mere prescription to heal what ails the preacher's performance. Cressman invites nothing less than the renewal of the art of preaching in our time through the renewal of the preacher's soul for the sake of the Gospel. Through the integration of one's own life and spirituality into this vessel called a sermon, Cressman invites each reader and practitioner to discover that we ourselves are Good News."

—The Rt. Rev. C. Andrew Doyle
Episcopal Diocese of Texas
Author of *The Jesus Heist: Recovering the Gospel from the Church*

" 'You're the only one who knows God the way you do, the only one who can reveal God to us the way you can.' This is the heart of this book on preaching. So much literature on homiletics focuses on the homily and ignores the homiletician. The Rev'd Cressman offers us a book that gives a word of grace into this omission."

—Tripp Hudgins
Bogard Teaching Fellow, Church Divinity School of the Pacific
Berkeley, California

"This an honest book offering real hope. I look forward to using the big insights of this little book with both beginning and seasoned preachers."

—Gregory Heille, OP, professor of preaching and evangelization,
Aquinas Institute of Theology

# Backstory Preaching

*Integrating Life, Spirituality, and Craft*

The Rev'd Lisa Kraske Cressman

Foreword by Gregory Heille, OP

**LITURGICAL PRESS**

Collegeville, Minnesota

www.litpress.org

Cover design by Monica Bokinskie. Image courtesy of Getty Images.

Scripture quotations are from New Revised Standard Version Bible © 1989 National Council of the Churches of Christ in the United States of America. Used by permission. All rights reserved worldwide.

© 2018 by Order of Saint Benedict, Collegeville, Minnesota. All rights reserved. No part of this book may be reproduced in any form, by print, microfilm, microfiche, mechanical recording, photocopying, translation, or by any other means, known or yet unknown, for any purpose except brief quotations in reviews, without the previous written permission of Liturgical Press, Saint John's Abbey, PO Box 7500, Collegeville, Minnesota 56321-7500. Printed in the United States of America.

| 1 | 2 | 3 | 4 | 5 | 6 | 7 | 8 | 9 |
|---|---|---|---|---|---|---|---|---|

**Library of Congress Cataloging-in-Publication Data**

Names: Cressman, Lisa Kraske, author.
Title: Backstory preaching : integrating life, spirituality, and craft / the Rev'd Lisa Kraske Cressman.
Description: Collegeville, Minnesota : Liturgical Press, 2018.
Identifiers: LCCN 2017053406 (print) | LCCN 2018016773 (ebook) | ISBN 9780814645383 (ebook) | ISBN 9780814645147
Subjects: LCSH: Preaching.
Classification: LCC BV4211.3 (ebook) | LCC BV4211.3 .C76 2018 (print) | DDC 251—dc23
LC record available at https://lccn.loc.gov/2017053406

*To my husband, Erik.*
*Thank you not only for my "seven years,"*
*but for more than thirty years of best friendship;*

*and,*

*to my Dad,*
*children's book author many times over,*
*Robert L. Kraske.*
*When I was a child you taught me the value of the written word*
*and to trust my voice*
*every time you asked me to edit your manuscripts.*
*It's high time a book were dedicated to you.*

# Contents

# foreword

This book about the preaching life doesn't shy away from the real stresses of a parish preacher's life. This is an honest book offering real hope.

With twenty-five years in the pulpit, Lisa Kraske Cressman knows firsthand the demons that can beset preachers who must produce yet one more sermon (and, for many preachers, so many more) each week. She compares the predicament of an early-career preacher to that of an imaginary violinist being told to play to a concert hall after only one year of studying violin. With one or two seminary courses in preaching, countless preachers are bewildered or overwhelmed as eyes and ears turn expectantly to them once again as they step into the pulpit. Speaking to preachers, Cressman writes:

> When we graduate, though, the expectations are high. We're expected to play the violin beautifully, energetically, and in tune. We're expected to be expressive and creative, and improvise our own tunes on the spot for our listeners, just for them. And, we are expected—and expect ourselves—to do this every week, without further critique, coaching, or guidance.

A seasoned preacher knows that the preaching craft requires years of week-in, week-out work. To this end preachers need some help—which is precisely the coaching and guidance that Cressman offers at her backstorypreaching.com website and in this, her first book. But let the reader of this book be aware: the authenticity of Cressman's coaching and guidance stems from her honest confession that no preacher can sustain the discipline of the pulpit without first, and in an ongoing way, experiencing a person-to-person, transforming encounter with the living Word of God.

Cressman's essential call to the spiritual life takes preachers to the very roots or origins of their Christian vocation. Pope Francis preached about this at the second Easter Vigil of his papacy when he said, "Go back to Galilee":

> For each of us, too, there is a "Galilee" at the origin of our journey with Jesus. "To go to Galilee" means something beautiful, it means rediscovering our baptism as a living fountainhead, drawing new energy from the sources of our faith and our Christian experience. To return to Galilee means above all to return to that blazing light with which God's grace touched me at the start of the journey. From that flame I can light a fire for today and every day, and bring heat and light to my brothers and sisters. That flame ignites a humble joy, a joy which sorrow and distress cannot dismay, a good, gentle joy.[1]

This good, gentle joy is the joy of the Gospel that lies at the heart of Christian discipleship and at the heart of the preaching life. We often are privileged to see this joy being lived by our parishioners in the midst of the suffering and the immense pressures of their day-to-day discipleship. And, if we can be honest, sometimes it is we the preachers and the ministers who want what so many of our parishioners have—a personal relationship with Jesus and a rock-solid experience of the joy of the Gospel. Like our parishioners, we are called to joyful, intentional discipleship.

Not only does Rev'd Cressman reacquaint preachers with this deep thirst for the very sources of discipleship; she also takes the opportunity to patiently teach preachers a time-tested practice for slaking this thirst: *lectio divina*.

In a way, while Cressman writes from within her Episcopalian context and never mentions Pope Francis, the whole of *Backstory Preaching: Integrating Life, Spirituality, and Craft* can be read as an unpacking of the following two paragraphs of Francis in his apostolic exhortation *Evangelii Gaudium* (The Joy of the Gospel):

---

1. Pope Francis, homily for the Easter Vigil (Rome, Vatican Basilica, April 19, 2014 [Holy Saturday]), at www.vatican.va.

Preparation for preaching is so important a task that a prolonged time of study, prayer, reflection and pastoral creativity should be devoted to it. . . . Some pastors argue that such preparation is not possible given the vast number of tasks which they must perform; nonetheless, I presume to ask that each week a sufficient portion of personal and community time be dedicated to this task, even if less time has to be given to other important activities. . . . A preacher who does not prepare is not "spiritual"; he is dishonest and irresponsible with the gifts he has received.

. . . To interpret a biblical text, we need to be patient, to put aside all other concerns, and to give it our time, interest and undivided attention. We must leave aside any other pressing concerns and create an environment of serene concentration. It is useless to attempt to read a biblical text if all we are looking for are quick, easy and immediate results. Preparation for preaching requires love. We only devote periods of quiet time to the things or the people whom we love; and here we are speaking of the God whom we love, a God who wishes to speak to us. Because of this love, we can take as much time as we need, like every true disciple: "Speak, Lord, for your servant is listening" (1 Sam 3:9).[2]

Preachers who patiently commit themselves to a daily contemplative practice of *lectio divina* will joyfully and readily be able to give to others the Gospel fruits of their contemplation. Cressman not only makes this promise to her readers; she also takes her readers by the hand as they learn the Christian practices for doing so.

Like Cressman, Pope Francis also realizes that good preaching is not so much about oratorical skill as it is about prayer and about being transformed in a loving encounter with God:

Whoever wants to preach must be the first to let the word of God move him deeply and become incarnate in his daily life. In this way preaching will consist in that activity, so intense and fruitful, which is "communicating to others what one has contemplated." . . . Today too, people prefer to listen to witnesses: they "thirst for authenticity" and "call for evangelizers to speak of a God whom

---

2. Pope Francis, Post-Synodal Apostolic Exhortation on the Proclamation of the Gospel in Today's World (*Evangelii Gaudium*), November 24, 2013, pars. 145–46.

they themselves know and are familiar with, as if they were seeing him." (*Evangelii Gaudium*, 150)

I look forward to using the big insights of this little book with both beginning and seasoned preachers. These chapters show how the venerable Christian practice of *lectio divina* can help transform inexperienced, harried, or even burned-out preachers into disciples and evangelists brimming over with love of God and the joy of ministering the Gospel—preachers who can say with the psalmist:

> I am like a green olive tree
>    in the house of God.
> I trust in the steadfast love of God
>    forever and ever.
> I will thank you forever,
>    because of what you have done.
> In the presence of the faithful
> I will proclaim your name, for it is good. (Ps 52:8-9)

Gregory Heille, OP
Professor of preaching and evangelization
Aquinas Institute of Theology, St. Louis

# Acknowledgments

I never set out to write a book, nor did I set out to create a ministry to serve my fellow preachers. But the Holy Spirit has a funny way of using the isolation of the metaphorical desert to build something new, even when—perhaps especially when—nothing can be seen in any direction on the horizon to walk toward. The Holy Spirit, then, gets all the credit for this book and planting in me the idea for Backstory Preaching, an idea so startling and unforeseen that it jerked me awake from a deep sleep in the heart of a winter's night.

Each person who listened and took a chance to bring this ministry and book to life deserves profound credit for their intrepidness and trust.

Credit goes first to the Episcopal Diocese of Texas, including the Bishop, the Rt. Rev'd C. Andrew Doyle, the Canon to the Ordinary, the Rev'd Kai Ryan, and the Rev'd Beth Fain, none of whom thought the idea for Backstory Preaching was too far "out there" and facilitated the next steps. Credit is due too to the Bishop Quin Foundation who offered the seed money to launch this ministry. Together you afforded me the most exciting and fitting ministry opportunity I can imagine. Thank you.

The first two classes of the Backstory Preaching Mentorship, the Apprentices, and my partners, the Rev'd Micah Jackson, PhD, the Rev'd Cathie Caimano, Ms. Shaundra Taylor, and Ms. Mary Cromack—what can I say? You helped form and shape this ministry and pressed upon me the need to write for you what was swirling in my head. Without you, literally, this book would not exist. Thank you for your patience, perseverance, encouragement, and invaluable feedback, and especially for your friendship. I couldn't do this work without you.

# Introduction

It's Monday morning. I walk through the door of my church office determined to get an early start on my sermon. I glance at the Scripture lessons for next Sunday and groan: *The Good Shepherd? Again?* I slump in my chair wondering what in the world there is left to say about shepherds, sheep, pastures, and name-calling. I've said it all before.

Still, I buck up my resolve. *I can do this!* I will start fresh because I *will not* spend another night like *that* one, even though the nights like *that* one seem to number like the stars.

*That* night is the night before preaching, the night I'm too often thrust into "The PPZ: the Preacher's Panic Zone." That's the night I spend frozen like the proverbial deer in the headlights, staring at the blinking computer cursor, willing it to form pixels into letters, inklings into stories, and vague memories of seminary studies into profound theological insights that don't materialize, in search of yet another elusive sermon message.

The nights before preaching aren't supposed to be spent that way. They're supposed to be spent relaxing like other people do. Pizza, popcorn, and Netflix would be heaven! Instead, those evenings may not be spent in hell, but they're at least spent in purgatory while I wait. I wait to be set free from the panic of walking to the pulpit, hundreds of eyes on me, and opening my mouth without a single brilliant syllable prepared to emerge. All it would take is for the Spirit to make the message materialize on the screen. I could take it from there.

Would that it worked that way! I stand up and walk to my window. If only I had been born with a *gift* for preaching like those famous preachers who preach beautifully and effortlessly, who always say something that moves people, something that *matters*! Thank God, at least, my colleagues don't hear me. I'd wither inside if they did.

But that was then and this is now, a fresh Monday morning, when I link arms with St. Peter and offer my third denial in as many minutes: *Not anymore. I'm not heading into the PPZ ever again.* Hearing myself gives me pause: *Do I, like you, Peter, protest too much?* I nudge aside my misgivings to make room for my gleaming, renewed intentions and set them on my desk next to my coffee cup. I stretch to the ceiling and ease into my office chair again. No more procrastinating, I'll have it finished with time to spare, so help me God!

I return to the text. My eyes glide over the lesson again. I breathe deeply and ask the Holy Spirit to guide me. My mind focuses. *Sheep. Right. Shepherd. Yup. Sheepfold? Maybe . . . nah. Called by name? Did that last year.* My spirits droop. Adrenaline begins its warm-up jog in my gut. *Oh, no,* as I close my eyes, *not again!* I have no leads. I got nothin'.

Well, I *have* gotten an early start on my sermon. That's something, anyway. Now that I know what the lesson is, maybe I can ruminate on it. Sure, like sheep ruminate on their cud. (*Or is that cows? Is there something about ruminating that could be a sermon?*) I'll come back fresh tomorrow. There's still plenty of time.

But then, there are the expected unexpected meetings, pastoral visits, and sundry parish crises. I know I should spend time on the sermon, but it's almost impossible to make the time when so many other things have to be done. And it's not just finding the time. I know I should try harder, dig deeper, look for the tracks, find that dry footprint that indicates the Good Shepherd passed by some time back. If I could just hunt him down to hear the message he wants me to give! I guiltily put other demands off to spend a couple of hours searching for him, but I can't find him and he doesn't send a messenger to give me his coordinates. *Really, Jesus? Couldn't you help a poor preacher out?* I whisper.

It's now my Sabbath day. I should be re-creating my spirit, but instead I'm spending the morning translating Greek, listening to sermon podcasts, and perusing sermon links online. I'm tempted to pull a brilliant sermon off the internet, but I'm not that desperate yet. (Besides, were my congregation to hear a "brilliant" sermon, I fear they would question its origins.) I keep trying but I can't find that "nugget," that glint of gold that signals the "eureka" moment when a sermon message is about to be revealed. A headache and knotted shoulders tell me it might be better if I were to take a break and leave the house to run some errands. *Or am I just procrastinating?* Refusing to answer, stomach fluttering, I give up on the sermon for the rest of the day.

Stuff happens, time flies, and it's now crunch time. I search for my favorite mug and fuss to make the perfect cup of coffee. Now, with nothing left between me and the last sign I had of the Good Shepherd's trail, I give in to the inevitable. I know what's ahead. Hard work. Lonely work. And it's going to take hours.

I don't know whether this makes it better or worse, but I believe the sermon matters. I want a great sermon because I want to share Good News, because I love God, and I love my people. I want them to receive a message of hope, love, forgiveness, and joy. My people matter and the Gospel matters, so my sermon *matters*! For that reason I want to deliver a *great* sermon, but, at this point, I'd settle for a passable one. One with an actual message. That I don't yet have. *An internet sermon . . . ?*

*Here it is again,* I sigh. *The Preacher's Panic Zone.*

Does the task of preaching sometimes feel like not such good news, like it does for this preacher? But what if it did? What if the opportunity to preach every Sunday felt like *Great* News? To make preaching every week feel like great news, it would probably require that we felt renewed by sermon prep instead of drained by it. It would probably require that our eyes didn't roll with boredom by the same Scripture lessons, but instead, widened in wonder to encounter the Gospel anew, even in the all-too-familiar stories. It would probably require, too, that the message felt revealed instead of wrested from the text, and we felt confident we knew how to craft that message effectively every week. And finally, to make preaching feel like great news, sermon prep wouldn't be buried by other priorities, because preaching *was* the priority.

That's what this book is about. This book identifies why preaching doesn't always feel like such good news to the preacher and gets practical about overcoming those obstacles. That's one promise. But this book promises more. It also shows how to integrate life and spirituality with the craft of preaching to make us the most authentic, awestruck preachers we can be.

What obstacles am I referring to? There are two sets. Let's talk about the second set first. These are the obstacles we have to overcome to develop proficient preaching skills. If you went to a traditional seminary, the complexity and depth of each subject is so massive that most of us know when we graduate we're still in our infancy of learning. And perhaps for no subject is this more true than preaching. That starts with the fact that preaching is the only theological discipline that applies *every* other discipline. (That is, one can be a New Testament scholar without preaching, but one can't preach without being a New Testament scholar.) That means every subject that lacks depth of knowledge exponentially multiplies our ignorance for preaching.

Not only do we have to rely on all the other theological disciplines, we have to learn about preaching itself: what it is, what it isn't, and how to do it. We have to know the difference between a speech, an inspirational talk, and a sermon; how to conduct exegesis and apply hermeneutics; and when, for example, a pastoral sermon is called for compared to a prophetic one. That's aside from developing the skills of expression needed to preach a single, clear message that keeps listeners on the edge of their seats and sends them off equipped to live more of the Good News this week than they were last. Preaching is extraordinarily complex and requires more time, training, and feedback than any seminary has the time to accomplish.

Through no fault of our seminaries, we are so accustomed to swimming in this ocean of insufficient preaching training we don't recognize it for what it is. To put the limitations of our training in context, let's compare it to learning a different skill, like the violin, and instead of seminary, we're at a sacred music school. Let's be generous and assume we can read music before we arrive and are allotted two semesters for violin training. The first semester we learn a little about the violin's history, why it's played in church, how to hold the violin and apply the bow, and scratch out our first three-note tune. The second semester we learn to caterwaul our first seven-note tune and manage our nerves when we complete the requirements to play twice at church and three times in front of our class, each time haltingly and out of tune. The only coaching and critique we receive from our teacher is the three times we play in class.

When we graduate, though, the expectations are high. We're expected to play the violin beautifully, energetically, and in tune. We're expected to be expressive and creative, and improvise our own tunes on the spot for our listeners, just for them. And, we are expected—and expect ourselves—to do this every week, without further critique, coaching, or guidance.

Truly, as preachers we hope against any hope to preach well because the deficiency in our training is nearly as equal as learning to play the violin in two semesters. Our lack of training compared to the expectations is as ludicrous as it is unrecognized.

Moreover, this problem isn't limited to new grads. It doesn't matter how much experience you have or how many times you've been in the pulpit; if you don't take that seven-note tune and practice diligently and intentionally, and no one gives you the tools you lack to get better at it, how can you? If you're only repeating over and over again the little you know, it's no wonder the thought of achieving excellence in preaching can feel like a hopeless undertaking, as if the Holy Spirit passed you by to give the "gift" of preaching to someone else.

Speaking of which, with all due respect to the Holy Spirit, the vast majority of those who preach proficiently are made, not born, because of three things. First, they pay attention to their craft and work at it with deliberate practice and feedback. Second, they keenly observe life: God's, their listeners', and their own. And third, they are intentional about growing in their relationship with God aside from being a preacher.

This segues into the first set of obstacles to preach proficiently, and that is—well, I don't know another way to say this other than to say it. The first set of obstacles is us, the preachers. That's because writing a sermon starts with *us*. A sermon starts with us as baptized children of God and with what each of us believes is the Good News. A sermon starts with us and our backstories because that's the venue in which the Spirit creates a message. Our whole selves walk into the pulpit. No part of us can be left out, and no part of the Gospel can be filtered out of the image of God we represent and its incarnation through our experience, education, and ministry context.

The backstory of your preaching is how you understand God for yourself. That backstory helps you articulate what you know of the Good News in the form of a sermon, because here's the short of it: if you don't believe the Good News *yourself*, if you haven't experienced God revealed in the text *for yourself* so you *know* it to be true, then why should your listeners trust what you proclaim? (And lest you feel nervous that I am abdicating tradition and responsible scholarship and exegetical method, fear not!) Consistently effective preachers, then, not only work to overcome obstacles to develop their skills, they also submit themselves to the Holy Spirit so the obstacles in themselves are as few as possible, and they are made into the Word of God they preach.

Many preachers we naively label as "gifted," then, in fact reveal truly Good News: *Consistently effective, awestruck preaching can be learned by every preacher who intentionally practices the craft of preaching and integrates it with their backstory and spirituality.* Regardless of the amount or type of training we received, or how recent or long ago it was, we can learn to preach ever more effectively and with enthusiasm. And we can do so not only without the stress and weekly drama, but in the process of sermon prep, be renewed for our lives and ministries. We can all be confident, proficient, perpetually wonder-filled preachers.

If this is what you long for, do these three things: pray, read this book, and do the exercises. Because deep change and skill development happens only through slow, deliberate, focused practice, there's a workbook to accompany this book. You'll find it on the Backstory Preaching website at www.backstorypreaching.com.

The chapters of this book weave back and forth: One chapter about who you are—that is, your backstory as a child of God who happens to have been called to preach. The next, how to pray your sermon into being, so that you, the preacher, publicly proclaim the living God you know. The backstory chapters integrate your life and spirituality with your preaching, in particular by looking at the obstacles into which many of us fall. Obstacles like perfectionism and seeing sermons as products rather than prayer. Obstacles like not really, truly believing you're loved, and preaching in ways to protect yourself from negative reactions. Obstacles like seeing preaching as a check mark on the weekly to-do list rather than the extraordinary gift it is to *read God,* so extraordinarily so, that you *can't wait* to tell your people what you read of God this week! And obstacles like those represented in the preacher in the opening scenario—procrastination, Scripture fatigue, and not believing what you have to say matters, while trusting what you have to offer is enough.

The preaching chapters dovetail by slowly unfolding a spirituality infused sermon prep process in which you abide and discover *new* Good News to transform you. Though this is not a new prayer method—indeed, it is approaching nigh on sixteen hundred years old—it may be new to you as a way to approach sermon prep. *Lectio divina* helps you discover a message of Good News you know is true because you experienced it. (Again, if you're feeling nervous and think *lectio divina* can't contain the sound scholarship of tradition and reason, I'll ask you to read the book, then think yet again.) *Lectio divina* integrates your life and spirituality with the craft of preaching. The stages of *lectio divina*, explained later, are prayerful states of mind to combine prayer, responsible scholarship, skill development, and the delightful element of holy surprise.

The final chapter puts it all together, your backstory with your preaching, and your life and spirituality with your craft. You'll be asked to think and pray deeply about developing as a preacher and then go beyond the thinking and praying to write a trust: a Preacher's Trust. The Preacher's Trust is an actual document you write and sign, to share and declare your intentions and practices to be Good News in order to preach Good News.

Finally, I want you to know the scriptural, organizing principle I have around preaching. With my whole being, I believe this is what we are called to do each and every time we proclaim the Good News:

"We declare to you what was from the beginning, what we have heard, what we have seen with our eyes, what we have looked at and touched with our hands, concerning the word of life—this life was revealed, and we have seen it and testify to it, and declare to you the eternal life that was with the Father and was revealed to us—we declare to you what we have seen and heard so that you also may have fellowship with us; and truly our fellowship is with the Father and with his Son Jesus Christ. We are writing these things so that our joy may be complete" (1 John 1:1-4).

May it ever be so.

# CHAPTER ONE

# Preaching Isn't Performance, It's Prayer

### Good News

The Good News is, through the Holy Spirit,
sermons are prayer,
not product.

### Prayer

I pray you see that when you focus on the Good News in your own life,
you can preach the Good News for all lives.

### Problem

We perform to protect ourselves.

### Vision

When your sermon prep shifts the focus from product to prayer,
Christ reveals the Good News through you to everyone.

### Chapter in a Sentence

First, we're formed; then, the sermon is.

### Latch

A story

(The workbook to integrate this chapter with your backstory and preaching
can be found at www.backstorypreaching.com.)

## Backstory

*When they had prayed, the place in which they were gathered
together was shaken; and they were all filled with the Holy Spirit
and spoke the word of God with boldness (Acts 4:31).*

The mountains! Who can't find God in gorgeous places like the
Rocky Mountains? The quiet, craggy, colossal magnificence of them!
The perpetual fluttering fans of billions of golden Quaking Aspen
leaves! Who isn't moved to fall to their knees to sense the presence
of God in such a place?

Uhh, that would be me.

Well, more accurately, I didn't find God where I *expected* to find
God in the mountains. I found God easily enough in the mountains in
Utah on the trails I hiked and ran as often as I could. Where I didn't
find God was in the church in the mountains in Utah. Or, to get to
the real point, I didn't find God in the preacher in the church in the
mountains in Utah.

Right after college I lived in the mountains above the Salt Lake City
valley for four years. While there, I attended a tiny Episcopal church
of about twelve members. A hospital chaplain served as our regular
Sunday supply priest. He was a great guy, ordained for twenty years
or so. Pastoral. Smart. Caring. Intellectual. *Very* intellectual.

I attended that church for a while but then drifted elsewhere. Three
months later, a member of that church asked me to tell her why I had
left. After I hemmed and hawed for a bit, she asked me to be blunt.
So I was blunt (and presumptuous): "I don't feel like the priest has
a prayer life. I don't feel like he has any connection to the One he's
preaching about."

It turned out that member was a good friend of the priest's. She
felt she needed to tell him about my comments because he was the
kind of person who would want to know. He would want to grow
and learn if there were something to grow and learn from.

She told him, and it turned out I'd been right.

He didn't have a prayer life. He hadn't prayed regularly in years.
He didn't read Scripture other than for sermon prep. He had fallen
into a preaching pattern that allowed him to rely on his considerable
intellect. He could preach about his subject. Or really, he could *talk*
about his subject. He talked about Jesus in the same way as if he were
examining fascinating characteristics of the Quaking Aspen. It was as

if he were standing on the street looking at the trees from a distance, vaguely remembering climbing the trails to be surrounded by their shimmering, gold leaves. Listening to him preach about Jesus as if he had once known him a long time ago didn't work for me.

I needed to hear preaching from someone who knew God. Not someone who had once *known* God. Not someone who knew *about* God. I needed to hear from someone who would recognize Jesus if he ran into him on the trail. I needed to hear how the preacher knew that Jesus was still alive because they had broken their fast together that morning over rainbow trout and an open fire in the Wasatch Mountains. I needed to hear his stories about Jesus going ahead of him to wait for him along with the summer grazing sheep, in the meadow so high up the White Pine Trail that they could look down on the tops of the aspens and fall silent over the beauty. I also needed to hear some explanation why, after seeing Jesus in the meadow once, Jesus didn't show up again as anticipated . . . as hoped for. I needed to dip my toe into the stream of trust that Jesus loved me if for no other reason than the preacher had learned in those encounters that Jesus loved him.

But this is not what the preacher preached, and I sensed he didn't know who he was talking about. As smart as the preacher was and as clear as his messages were, and as much as I trusted his scholarly and human integrity, I didn't trust his sermons because he didn't know his subject.

To integrate spirituality with craft, preachers need to know their divine subject intimately. That's why preachers pray. We want people to trust our sermons because they know the One we're talking about. We need to prevent our own sad slip into the theoretical because we haven't experienced the divine person. We need to prevent the hardening of our hearts that happens when Jesus becomes an *idea* instead of the living God.

Most of the time we have to be cautious about assumptions, but I think a fair one is our congregations expect and assume their preachers pray. I've never surveyed congregations to ask whether they actually hold this assumption so my own assumption could be wrong, but, I mean, don't *you* expect and assume that preachers pray?

Our listeners are right to expect us to set aside time to pray. To pray for them, for the church and the world, and especially, as the old story goes, "to look at the good God while the good God looks at me." To look at the good God is what forms us most as preachers.

Without regular, steady prayer, we lose our "why," our raison d'être, our leitmotif for preaching. If lose touch with the One we preach about, we don't know who we're talking about anymore and listeners' trust in our preaching declines.

To know *about* is not the same as to know for oneself, and it is to know God for oneself that gives preachers credibility. Yes, of course, there is the authority of the church which gives us credibility and the authority to preach at all, and I do not discount that. But neither the authority of the church, nor our degrees and education, nor the number of sermons we have offered mean a thing if we don't fall to our knees in awe of God. If we don't, we preach like clanging symbols instead of preaching like the living, loving Christ. Indeed, the relationship with God most conducive to preaching is vibrant, perpetual, cellular, evolving, and never to be taken for granted. We rely on Christ to be, exist, breathe, notice, question, doubt, ponder and understand, and only then to craft and preach.

So, prayer is our own "oxygen mask" that we put on before we can help others, because it reminds us of our *why*: why we are, why we were baptized, why we accepted a call to serve God in the church, and in some places, why we risk our lives to do so.

"But," you might protest, "who has time? There's so much work to do! If I pray for half an hour, there are vitally important things that won't get done!"

No, they won't. Not even Jesus got it all "done."

Think of the work Jesus left "undone." Widows still begged. Orphans still slept in the streets. And the number of people who were poor, powerless, and vulnerable to the Romans on the day Jesus was born was the same number on the day Jesus died.

And yet, Jesus took time to pray. Jesus still walked away *from* the needs of others *for* the needs of others. What allowed Jesus to preach, heal, teach, and verbally spar with his adversaries was his connection to his Father. His connection to God gave him the wisdom to discern what he ought to do next, the strength to carry it out, and the self-compassion to trust he had done enough for one day, even with so much left to do.

Of course, he left us to complete his work, with the help of the Holy Spirit and one another. He did finish his work by entrusting us with the balance, to preach, heal, teach, and confront the powers that be. Jesus left us the work to complete the reign of God on earth until he returns, and regularly conduct ourselves the way he did: to walk away, be alone, and pray while there is still work to be done.

The argument you may raise is that we have a schedule but Jesus didn't. As far as we know, Jesus didn't have a daily planner. If Jesus lived a schedule like ours, his day might have gone like this: "9:00, Disciples' Meeting," followed by "9:30, Preach. 10:00–3:00, Feed Five Thousand." The feeding ran late (people stayed behind to talk to Jesus, so he didn't get out of there until 3:56). Because of that, his "3:30, Heal Ten Lepers" session started late, too, which also took longer than expected. Supper with his mom was nonnegotiable and he had to commute an hour each way, so by the time he walked back to the disciples, Jesus was beat and the day was done. A few mumbled prayers to God as he drifted off to sleep were as much as he managed.

I'm guessing, but I don't think that's how Jesus managed his time with God or his ministry.

Jesus didn't need a daily planner but he was just as busy without one, and anytime he prayed, he was leaving ministry "undone." People standing around the camels in the camel corral probably complained about him for not tending to their every need the same way our parishioners do about us in church parking lots. *Jesus prayed anyway.*

Eventually, so did the preacher of my mountain church. More for his sake than for my own, I am happy to tell you I returned to the tiny church in Utah a few months after the priest started to pray again. He stopped protecting himself from the vulnerable intimacy of deep gnosis with God. He let himself be seen by God through prayer and Scripture, over coffee, the newspaper, and art. He came to know Jesus again and was changed by the encounters, and his sermons changed accordingly. Now, rather than conveying a sense that he stood apart from Jesus, there was a gentleness in his demeanor. It was as if he had brought his long-lost friend with him to church, a friend whom he was both eager to introduce and a bit shy to reveal, knowing that in the revelation of his friend he would also reveal something of himself.

That priest's sermons were still really smart. But they also became beautiful, because they told us something new the priest had learned in the past week about his old friend that rather caught him by surprise. His sermons seemed to say, "Hmmm. Who knew? I thought you'd want to know too."

I did.

## *From Protection to Performance to Prayer*

Eyes avert. Lids conceal. Cheeks flush. Words bump and clutch with "umms," pauses, and diversionary explanations, as if the conversation were learning to drive a stick shift.

No matter how proficient the preacher, this is usually the preamble I see leading up to talking about their sermons. The more certain they feel about the sermon, the more averting, concealing, flushing, and clutching I see.

It's understandable; I read this way, too. Preaching is one of the most vulnerable things we do. We expose our smarts, spirits, and selves in a sermon. As we walk to the pulpit, we might worry, *Does this sermon say anything worthwhile? Did I do that piece of exegesis right? What will people think of me? What would my bishop think of my theology? How will the "church tradition police" react to this? Am I going to put people to sleep? Or worse, make them mad? Oh, my God! what's my colleague doing here? He's going to think I'm such an idiot!* For some preachers, only the occasional sermon is fraught with anxiety. For others, every single one is.

We reveal so much of ourselves in sermons that some preachers feel embarrassed for having preached an *effective* one. Even though they never say the word "I," they feel as though too much of their insides have been put on display. Because we share in public what we hold most sacred, preaching can feel as intimate as broadcasting a personal secret.

Yes, sermons make us feel vulnerable, but what about that vulnerability? What makes us feel exposed? What do we risk? What do we risk if we knock one out of the park? What do we risk if we strike out?

Here's the good news, but the good news is so simple it's hard to believe. What's at risk? The Good News, the Best News, for preachers is, what we risk is not what we fear most. *That is, the union God forged with us through Christ is not at risk.* God bound himself to us through Jesus, and that binding will never be strengthened, loosened, or severed based on the quality of our sermons. Your best sermon doesn't make God proud so that you're rewarded with your place card moved next to Jesus' at the next family supper, nor does your worst sermon make God want to banish you to your bedroom with a TV dinner. Your place at the table is already next to Jesus, the same as it always was, is now, and always will be.

The Good News is, what's most important is not at risk. Yet, if that were easy to believe, we would already. Why don't we? Our bodies sometimes reveal that we believe there's a lot at risk. We get clues whenever we flush with pride from a compliment, feel the glow of our own cleverness, or gaze from on high from the top-of-the-heap of our imaginary sermon competition. Or, when we shrink from embarrassment, are crushed by shame, or rush to the nearest hidey-hole, our bodies are telling us we believe there's more at risk in our sermon than the propagation of the Gospel: We want God to think well of us. And sometimes we want people to think even better of us.

Preaching makes us vulnerable. It just does and there's no getting around it. Preaching is vulnerable because we reveal our most intimate beliefs; plus we're on public display, ready targets for people's opinions about everything from our vestments, tone of voice, hairstyle, weight, *and* our skills as a preacher.

To minimize our fears about parishioners' reactions, we might dress to specs, comb our hair, and draft sermon messages that rouse them to applause, or provoke only to the edge of withheld pledges. The problem is, as soon as we preach to protect or elevate ourselves, our preaching becomes tinged with performance, as if we were acting the part of a preacher. When we perform to protect ourselves, we're not preaching the Gospel we believe. We have, in fact, dis-integrated ourselves from God. We stand apart from the Source of holy words to preach the Gospel for a purpose: to prove we're worthy of others' regard.

Let me be personal for a moment. I feel vulnerable putting this book out to the public. I've never written a book, and I am little known in the preaching world. That causes me to wrestle mightily with the "Who do I think I am?" gremlin. I know I will receive a thumbs-down from some. I know some of those thumbs-down are not going to be from constructive criticism about these ideas, but rather, related to who I am. It happens to everyone who puts themselves out there. To make it worse, that criticism will come from people I've never met and with whom I have no relationship. I don't look forward to it.

The Good News is, I recognize my fear and vulnerability and don't want them to hold editorial sway over this book. What prevents me from caving to the negative reactions I fear is to write this book as one long prayer. One long prayer for you, your preaching, the people who hear you, and the spread of the Gospel.

What do I mean, this book is one long prayer? The *Book of Common Prayer* defines "prayer" as "responding to God, by thought and by deed, with or without words."[1] It's especially important to grasp that prayer is responding to God; it's never initiated by us. Jesus invites us perpetually to give our undivided attention, loyalty, and obedience to foster ever-deeper awareness of and trust in God's bond with us.

If prayer is a response to God, then this book is a response to God as a simultaneous offering of deed and word. In the same way, our preaching is a prayer when our preaching is a response to God's invitation to proclaim Good News.

Preaching is a response to *God,* and not to our real and imagined *critics,* when we re-member ourselves to God in prayer and Scripture, outside of the job to preach and lead worship. We need to sit with God in prayer to be reminded of Christ's choice to bind himself to us, to let ourselves be awash in mercy, compassion, respect, and love. We need to bring fully to mind again the most important thing there is: that to be God's forever-kin is not at risk. We also need to abide in Scripture to become newly aware that God is revealed most clearly through those who accepted the divine into their beings. Only by immersing ourselves in prayer and Scripture can we be formed until our sermons become prayer instead of a protective performance.

## Preaching

*"[L]et it be with me according to your word" (Luke 1:38).*

### Consent to Be Transformed through Prayer and Scripture, Daily

What reaction do you have to the idea of a daily prayer discipline? Do you look forward to it? Feel grateful? Excited? Pray without thinking because it's already a habit? Or do you groan, feeling like it's another item on the checklist? Do you steel yourself to the boredom? Do it because it's required of you? Or rebel against it for the same reason?

---

1. *Book of Common Prayer* (New York: Church Publishing, 1978), 856.

Or maybe you ignore it and pretend no one asks. I've felt all these at one point or another.

Although I don't have a reference, some years back the Lilly Foundation, one of the largest religious philanthropic organizations in the United States, wondered why many clergy didn't stay in ministry long enough to provide long-term stability to grow healthy congregations. They conducted a series of studies that eventually led to their "Pastoral Excellence Program."

One of their studies revealed this: most clergy don't pray. Harkening back to my priest at the beginning of this chapter, clergy felt the demands of ministry were overwhelming and they didn't have time. But for preachers, praying isn't in addition to the job; it *is* the job.

Not only is praying part of the preacher's job, prayer is in service of everything we do, including our preaching. Prayer integrates preaching with our life, and our life with preaching. All we are and everything we do reveals the Gospel because prayer is in service of *us*. Prayer is like a daily *Curious Case of Benjamin Button* when we reverse our age to return to the womb and Source of our being. Praying is our DNA's homecoming.

God yearns to get us all to Godself, to have it be just "I and Thou" for a bit. God might nudge us like a dad who says to his kid, "Hey, let's go for a walk, huh?" or a mom who says, "Let's play a game, just you and me." God's nudge doesn't always feel like a gentle invitation if we've set an alarm to pray and it intrudes when we're deep in the middle of a project. Just the same, God invites us because God wants to remind us of our divine-human bond. As we trust increasingly in that bond, we can preach that Good News of trust increasingly too. When we spend time with God, we are able to preach about someone we know. Not someone we know *about*, but someone we know very personally.

So, let me ask you this: Who is God? Not what you know of God from Scripture, though I know there are no sharp distinctions between categories. At the moment, I'm asking you to describe God (or Jesus or the Holy Spirit, whichever member of the Trinity you relate to most), whom you have come to know in *prayer*. God has revealed some part of Godself to you. Just as we can never know another person in totality, we can't know all of God. But what *do* you know? How would you describe God? How does God make Godself known to you? What are God's attributes, characteristics, mannerisms? How would you describe the status of your relationship?

This is the God you are probably describing in your sermons, whether you're aware of it or not. Through my prayer I know Jesus as compassionate, surprising, "un-pindownable," demanding, loyal, merciful, and funny. After long and consistent experience, I'm biased to see him this way in Scripture. That means I don't preach "hellfire and brimstone" sermons because I've never experienced him that way. (That also means I have to do extra work in my *meditatio* when Jesus is angry or speaks of bringing swords [Matt 10:34]).

Similarly, how would you describe God as you have learned about God in Scripture? As with prayer, to immerse ourselves in Scripture offers us the gift of knowing God. When we spend time inside those biblical stories, we remember how God bonded Godself to us. We remember that even though we screwed up, God reforged the bond with us anyway over and over, until God no longer needed a bond but became one with us through Jesus, end of story, beginning of story.

This brings me to *lectio divina* (Latin for "holy reading") and why I'm partial to it as a Bible study process for preachers. First, *lectio divina* keeps us "right-sized" as an average, typical, run-of-the-mill human being who happened to be called to preach. And second, *lectio divina* immerses us personally and intimately inside the One about whom we preach.

When we encounter average people in Scripture, we get reminded the *average* person is the summa cum laude of God's purposes. Few were exceptional unto themselves or displayed above-average intelligence, wit, or exceptional leadership. The majority were regular people who were probably good at some skills and lousy at others. Jesus called fishermen to be his first disciples. Yet Jesus, a carpenter, had to tell the "experts" which side of the boat to cast their nets to find the fish (Luke 5:4-6). These fishermen, who had probably fished since the time they could toddle into their dad's boat, weren't asked to follow Jesus because they would win any fishing contests. Think about Matthew and Zacchaeus, the Samaritan Woman at the well, Mary Magdalene and Mary, the Mother of our Lord. None was singled out because they had a particular skill set Jesus needed to fill out his leadership team and reshape the course of history.

Moreover, Jesus came from an average hamlet from an undistinguished family, and by the very absence of any remark about his carpentry skills, I infer they were literally unremarkable. Jesus wasn't even called "handsome," one of the distinguishing marks of God's favor in the Hebrew Scriptures. Indeed, those who were exemplary in the Bible, who did seem "above average," rose above the rest for one thing: faithfulness. In other words, their most distinguishing characteristic was not an *ability* but *trust*. They were exceptional in their sense of security in and their connection with God. When we pray Scripture through the four parts of *lectio divina*, we "embed" with these regular people who trusted God irregularly.

When we "hang out" with these people the result is to know we're not an exception to any rule. We are none other than the average human being who is skilled at some things and lousy at others, upon whom God took pity and is neither less nor more deserving of God's regard than anyone else. We do not stand outside the bounds of God's mercy, love, or compassion, nor are we special and get extras. No, we are just like all the other people in Scripture, and like all the people we preach to: human beings doing our best to make sense of life and God's work within it. We are no different from those in Scripture, nor are we different from the ones to whom we preach.

That brings us back to the second reason I'm partial to *lectio divina* for preachers: the first stage of *lectio divina*, *lectio* ("to read"), allows us to see biblical people just as they were and how God interacted with them. We notice, hear, and pay attention to them as if we were getting reacquainted with long-lost relatives. We pay close attention to what they said, how they dressed, what they ate, and what was left unsaid. This helps us understand our own faith-family history, but at first, only by gathering facts. We don't ascribe meaning to our observations, but catalog them with respect and compassion. In the same way that the observation of a photon will affect whether it is a particle or wave, when we first read the story we withhold judgments, conclusions, and assumed motivations so as not to affect the story as it was handed down to us.

*Lectio* is *really* hard for preachers. It's so hard this bears repeating. *Lectio is really hard for preachers* because we who preach are especially prone to assert meaning, to search for the "aha" that we hope signals the imminent arrival of a sermon message. And yet, when we rush the process, we miss so much! We miss the subtleties of the person's location, tone of voice, language play, and recurring themes. We also miss noticing those missing from the scene, those who don't speak, and words we gloss over for having read them so often. *Lectio* en-sconces us in the "micro" view of the story.

*Lectio divina* is so helpful to preachers that I also suggest *lectio divina* as our personal Bible study away from sermon prep because most of us need the extra practice to let Scripture be its own self. We need the practice to see these people as their own integral beings, that we enter their world as a guest, and to see that these people in Scripture weren't put on this planet for the purpose of providing us with a sermon two thousand years later. They lived their own lives with their own wants and desires, foibles and quirks, triumphs and revelations, and they deserve our respect as such. When we practice *lectio* as our own Bible study, we learn the value of doing the same in our sermon prep.

*Lectio* is the first stage of *lectio divina*. The second stage, *meditatio* (or "study"), is the hunt. *Meditatio* lets us wander down the rabbit holes of our curiosity. For example, in *meditatio*, we might pull out another translation to see whether a passage is worded the same way. We might wonder about a character and read her story from start to finish. We might be struck by the word "mercy" as if we've never seen it before and search the internet to find how many ways the Prodigal Son has been depicted in art, by whom, and when. We might also get curious about what's happening in our spirits when reading these stories. For example, compassion might arise in us while we listen to songs of laments, or burst with indignation when we stand next to those whose demand for answers from God went unrewarded, or swirl with confusion when we walk with those who wandered in deserts past their endurance. We might also wonder how and why God reacted to them the way God did? And how did Jesus respond? And why did the Holy Spirit's wind seem sometimes to blow only on the other side of the world?

When we hunt for answers and dig under the surface of the plot, we find these people's stories are our stories, stories in which "there is nothing new under the sun." Their stories of human existence are the same ones we tell today. Average stories of hope and death, promise and betrayal, insight and bewilderment, love, jealousy, forgiveness, war, unfairness, justice, and growing up. Stories of people doing their best, finding their way, hoping and trusting in God who didn't always make it easy for them to do so. Just like us. *Meditatio* lets us experience how normal the abnormal intervention of God-with-Us is.

*Oratio*, the next stage of *lectio divina*, is the "expression." During *meditatio*, we take in these stories and mush around in them until they become our own. But the process is not done if we hold them in. The insights need to be expressed, incarnated, made flesh. The expression becomes today's new Scripture, the new Scripture of this day's history of God with God's people, of God's history with you. This expression can be written, told, drawn, molded, sung, or stitched.

Finally, after *oratio* comes *contemplatio*, the last stage in which we "rest." We rest with God, sitting together in quiet, enjoying the very act of being together, of being amazed, of seeing the fruits of our shared time, and we are grateful. We see in the end that the best and truest part of life comes down to the simplest of acts: looking at the good God, and enjoying that the good God is looking at us.

I'll get more detailed about *lectio divina* in subsequent chapters, particularly as this ancient process is applied to praying a sermon into being. (If this is a new process to you, not to worry. You'll learn more about the how-tos shortly.) *Lectio divina* helps us know we are average, just like the people we read about. When we know we're just one more person through whom God does extraordinary things, we have nothing to prove in our sermons and no need to perform for the One who doesn't care whether we are average or not. God's bond with us is secure.

## Conclusion

To preach effectively and with integrity means to proclaim what we know. The best way to know God is through time spent apart together in prayer, and by dwelling in Scripture. Prayer and *lectio divina* are the wells to which we return again and again to help us remember our place, like the Samaritan woman. Like her, we come alone to the well to meet Jesus, to learn who he is so we can tell the others. We tell others the stories about God-with-Us because we have experienced and *know* God is with us. We have seen God, talked with Christ, and heard the Spirit tell us everything about ourselves. We are formed so we can form a sermon.

Prayer, *lectio divina*, and preaching make us vulnerable. They're risky because we don't know how God will reveal Godself to us, the impact the process will have, or what we will reveal about ourselves in the act of revealing God. And yet God, who meets us in prayer and *lectio divina*, makes us realize we have no need to protect ourselves with shield or buckler. We only have to tell the story God gives us to tell. That's enough for any average preacher.

# CHAPTER TWO

# An Effective Sermon

### *Good News*

The Good News is, effective sermons are sufficient to magnify the Lord.

### *Prayer*

I pray you see that
with intentional practice you can preach effectively week after week
and be transformed by Christ in the process.

### *Problem*

We lack the tools and support to practice and improve our preaching.

### *Vision*

All preachers engage in ongoing preaching formation
until they reach the level of proficiency to which they are called.

### *Chapter in a Sentence*

You can consistently discern, write, and offer
a clear message of Good News
authentic to you
and relevant to your listeners,
holding their attention
and inviting transformation.

### *Latch*

Definition

(The workbook to integrate this chapter with your backstory and preaching
can be found at www.backstorypreaching.com.)

## Backstory

*"My soul magnifies the Lord" (Luke 1:46).*

You know how we say some preachers have a "gift" for preaching? And intending to be kind, we also say about other preachers that preaching is not "their gift"? Neither is true. No preacher has a gift of preaching nor lacks one. I'm setting out to debunk this church legend that preaching is a "gift" at all.

Gifts of the Spirit for the church are mentioned in Paul's letters. Romans 12:6-8 lists these gifts as prophecy, ministry, teacher, exhorter, giver, leader, and the compassionate. First Corinthians 12:4-11 names them as uttering wisdom, having faith, the gift of healing, working of miracles, prophecy, discerning spirits, and various kinds of tongues. "Preaching" is not mentioned. In fact, an NRSV concordance search for "preaching" (and all its variations) reveals only fourteen entries, and none connects "gift" with "preaching."

With either pride or defeatism, the church legend we accept without question is that the Spirit predetermines who is gifted and who is not. It's as if we think the Spirit blows preaching dust on the foreheads of some preachers and not others to select a divine quota of gifted preachers per generation. We're either one of them or we're not, and if we're not, we're out of luck—or Spirit, as the case may be. No. According to Scripture preaching is not a "gift," and research suggests excellent preaching is possible for any preacher. If you feel skeptical about this claim, I refer you to the growing body of research about "talent" and "giftedness" in recent decades.[1] Let me summarize the research by saying that doubt is rising over the assumption that innate talent affects the heights of skill one can achieve. Indeed, compared to those who aren't born "talented" but work hard, the average-but-dedicated end up equally as acclaimed as those who are considered "gifted" or were "child prodigies." Heretical as this sounds, when you look deep into "talent," there's usually a vast trove of smart practice

---

1. For instance, I refer you to the fascinating book *Peak: Secrets from the New Science of Expertise,* by Anders Ericsson and Robert Pool (New York: Houghton Mifflin, 2016).

that was hitherto unknown or dismissed as inconsequential, including by people considered "natural" artistic geniuses, like Mozart.[2]

Consider the artistic genius of Maya Angelou, for example. I recall in an interview she said she resented it mightily when people dismissed her work as "easy" and "natural." Becoming more impassioned, she leaned forward in her chair, her face taut and voice level with frustration. She said something like, "People say to me, 'Of course you can write like that; you're Maya Angelou.'" Then she paused before continuing, "I work *hard* at my writing and at my poetry. I labor over it. It's never easy! Don't *ever* dismiss my efforts to make something *sound* beautiful and effortless."

Just as Ms. Angelou put in tremendous effort to sound like an effortlessly gifted writer, if you put in the work, you, too, are capable of sounding like an effortlessly gifted preacher. However, even though you are capable, that doesn't mean you are called to the same level of single-minded devotion as a Mozart or an Angelou, nor is it necessary. Gifted or great preaching isn't required for the propagation of the Gospel. Only *effective* preaching is, and effective preaching still requires intentional practice, hard work, and help. The rest of this book was written for you, the preacher who desires not only to be effective but to become ever *more* effective week after week, who wants to be spiritually nourished by the process, get sermons done in reasonable time, and without the weekly drama.

I hope you do want to become an ever more effective preacher and are willing to put in the effort. Just the same, I want to be sure we're clear on the contract you and I have regarding the rest of this book, and in no way do I intend my disclaimer to be insulting or patronizing. What I mean is this: the rest of this book gives you the tools to become a consistently effective preacher but you still have to pick them up and learn to use them. You have to pick them up, work through the awkward stages of unfamiliarity, modify them to fit your own hands, and finally become adept at their use. You have to put these suggestions into practice every time you preach. There are some suggestions that will make an immediate difference, while other skills will come slowly and become useful only when you practice

2. Ibid., loc. 61, Kindle.

consistently, evaluate, then practice again. If you do this reflective, intentional practice, however, you will become a consistently effective preacher. Meaning by definition that your sermons

offer a clear message of Good News
authentic to you,
relevant to your listeners,
holding their attention
and inviting transformation.[3]

This definition of an effective sermon is intentionally broad and promotes a process of sermon preparation that crosses denominational and theological borders. This definition contains the necessary bare bones of any sermon and, therefore, can offer a guideline to any preacher. Because each word or phrase means something in particular, let me "define the definition" further.

"Effective." Effective means *enough*. It gets the point across. It doesn't have to be oratory genius, perfection, or even "great" preaching. A solid message of hope, love, and forgiveness is sufficient unto the day to make and strengthen disciples. When we are faithful stewards of our time and energy, and avoid the harmful pursuit of "the perfect sermon," effective means *enough*.

"Sermon." A sermon is a unique liturgical craft. It's inspired by the Holy Spirit and combines the skills of writing and speech to interpret the Bible through the humanity, education, formation, and spirituality of the preacher to create living Scripture on behalf of a particular group of followers of Jesus Christ.

"Clear." The sermon can be followed from beginning to end with the skilled use of writing, transitions, and vocal inflections to offer a message a listener can summarize accurately in one sentence.

"Message." There is a point and purpose of, and meaning to, the sermon. The message is summarized by the preacher in "Good News," "Prayer," and "Vision" statements.

---

3. *Craft an Effective Sermon by Friday* ©Backstory Preaching, 2016. Used with permission.

"Good News." The Gospel of Jesus Christ extends to and invites us to be forgiven and changed by God's love, mercy, compassion, and faithfulness to us.

"Authentic." An authentic sermon is one that can only be preached with integrity by the one preacher.

"Preacher." A preacher is called and has been authorized by the church to interpret the Good News for a particular gathering of Jesus' disciples.

"Holding Their Attention." It isn't necessary to be witty, funny, or an exceptional writer to keep people listening. Questions, tension, and emotion draw people into the mystery too. A simple question like "Where is God?" can be sufficient to keep listeners on the edge of their seats.

"Relevant." A relevant message is pertinent. It matters to the particular gathering of Jesus' disciples.

"Listener." The listener is one who hears the sermon and is engaged enough to *hear it.*

"Inviting Transformation." What are we invited to move toward? What does the Promised Land look like? If the Good News is offering us something better than holding onto idols, the "Invitation to Transformation" describes what we have to look forward to after we say to God, "Let it be to me according to your word."

## Conclusion

Nearly all preachers need help because our preaching ministries are handicapped by minimal education in writing and preaching. To preach a consistently effective sermon requires a high skill level that is rarely mastered quickly.

Not only does effective preaching require time and effort to learn, to preach authentically requires time spent in prayer. Authentic preaching is formed through our relationship to God and as a prayer, or response, to God. By setting sermon prep in the context of prayer, the burden of outcome rests squarely where it belongs, with Christ. We do our part by showing up, opening up, and reading up, but Christ is the driver from the inspiration of ideas to the inspiration to hard work. It's all grace, and to apply that grace God requires our undivided attention and devotion.

I know, with Christ's help, our preaching will become more effective, and the Gospel spread farther to the glory of God, when we pray early and often; dive into Scripture for fun; read this book and integrate the concepts using the exercises in the workbook (www.backstorypreaching.com); and play with and mold these tools until they fit. This prayerful, reflective, integrative work can't help but make us all better preachers, inside and out.

# CHAPTER THREE

# Know You're Loved: The Gospel for Preachers

### *Good News*

The Good News is,
the quality of your sermon cannot make God love you more or less.

### *Prayer*

I pray you see
when you cultivate God's love for you, it'll preach.

### *Problem*

"I believe, Lord. Help thou my unbelief."

### *Vision*

The kingdom comes when you feel irresistibly drawn
to live, move, and have your being in God's love for you, every day.

### *Chapter in a Sentence*

You are loved, you are loved, you are loved.

### *Latch*

You can't outpace the rate of grace.

(The workbook to integrate this chapter with your backstory and preaching
can be found at www.backstorypreaching.com.)

## Backstory

*"I trust in the steadfast love of God,*
*    forever and ever"* (Ps 52:8).

*"As the Father has loved me, so I have loved you; abide in my*
*love"* (John 15:9).

If the statement were easy to believe, you'd believe it by now, right? You are loved. You are loved. *You are loved.*

With all God is and all God has, you are loved. There is no more love to be had, and there is none to be lost, and there is no more to be found. No matter how far, hard, and deep you might search for more, there is no holy grail of God's love yet to be discovered. There is no moldy book to be found in the bottom of a forgotten box on the bottom layer of a crumbled monastery in Budapest from the bottom of the thirteenth century that holds the faded map to the last hidden cache of God's love to be scraped from the bottom of the barrel. There isn't any more love to be found, because all there is has been given and it is in you, and you cannot contain any more of it than you already contain, because you have all there ever was, is, and will be. *All* of it.

You know this is true. You preach this love week in and week out. The sticking point is belief. If this much divine love were easy to accept, we would already. And, you, like me, probably don't believe. At least not fully. You, probably like me, believe only in part.

We have our moments. Moments when we believe fully, like the moment when we fully receive a loved one's proffered "I love you," and not because they're related to us. Or we have a moment when we taste consecrated bread and wine, and know if we'd been the only one ever to have tasted them, Jesus would still have gone to the cross for us. We have our moments when we are the resentful Elder Son standing outside the party next to his father and sense the twitch of his hand, hoping to hold our own. Yes, we have our moments.

What if we collected those moments, as if collecting moments when we know we are loved were a hobby? Like birders who keep binoculars at the ready, always prepared to notice and record bird sightings, how might we be changed if we always kept our hearts at the ready, always prepared to notice and record that we are loved?

The more we trained our hearts to notice and the more we recorded them, the more the pages would stack one on top of the other until it became a continuous flow, and one moment of being loved could no longer be distinguished from another. Were we to be so attuned and so believing, we would have found the Promised Land. We would be living in the reign of God.

Alas, none of us accepts God's love to its fullest. There's usually a diminuendo between the love God offers, the love we accept, and the love we extend in turn. Though it may sound naive and simplistic, I still think this is true: Why do any of us behave badly? Because we don't believe how much God loves us.

Why is this? Why don't we believe we are loved with all the love there is and then extend that love in a crescendo? There are as many explanations for that as there are people: Original sin. Family-of-origin issues. Abuse. Disrespectful comments that wound. Not fitting into molds. Personal failures. Never having been told we were loved, or having been told we weren't made lovable. Mental illness that doesn't let that knowledge take hold. All real. All hurtful. All conspire to compel us to deny the possibility.

All good reasons. But what if we chose to believe anyway? If we trusted in God's love fully even with all our "stuff," we wouldn't be interested to prove our worthiness through our preaching, by the size of our congregations, or by having the ears of denominational powers-that-be. If we lived in the Promised Land of Christ's love, we wouldn't yearn for anything or anyone other than Christ.

But we don't choose to place our faith in God's love, and we do try to prove our worthiness, and we do preen a little (on the inside, if not the out) with every powerful ear we bend. All of which gets in the way of our vocation to preach God's love—the love that we sincerely believe is for others, while denying divine love as an equal possibility for ourselves.

Yet oddly enough for a preacher, this has its advantages.

"You can't outpace the rate of grace."

So saith Sr. Mary Margaret Funk, OSB, during my spiritual direction sessions with her on more occasions you'd think would be necessary for me to grasp the concept.

"But why not?" I asked.

"Because until you're ready to say, like Mary, 'Let it be to me according to your word,' you're not ready. If you're not ready, you're not ready, and it's going to take its own time until you are."

*Dang.*

I didn't want grace to be "paced," as if I had to follow behind some kind of celestial pace car that set the slow speed toward glory. I wanted to zoom past and win the race *now*! I wanted the lightning-bolt routine: one huge zap of healing, grace, wisdom, and spiritual bliss! It would be for everyone's benefit, wouldn't it? I would be a better priest and preacher. More loving, forgiving, wise, and . . . *patient* . . . for the sakes of those I served. Truly, a win-win if ever there were one, right?

Fast, lightning-bolt epiphanies certainly work wonders at times; that's not to be denied. Mountaintop epiphanies can push us into big leaps of faith and change our lives and ministries for the better. But more often, brilliant epiphanies are about as effective in making lasting change as continuing education workshops: they're a terrific shot in the arm but rarely have lasting effects. Without the slow, sustained support and work to shift our hearts, minds, and spirits, we quickly return to the same old patterns. For example, there didn't seem to be much immediate change in the disciples after witnessing the transfiguration. Lasting change in them came after years of watching Jesus, witnessing his miracles, sitting at his feet to listen, asking questions, challenging him, praying with him, and going through agonizing, confusing times of his passion, death, and resurrection. It took the disciples three years before they truly came into their own. There must be a good reason God prefers that pedagogical method over a quick "zap," and it seems to be this: "Slow and steady wins the race."

The grace we cannot outpace is the rate of our acceptance and trust in the freedom to be truly loved as is, because there's only so much freedom we can stand. We need time to adjust to the freedom of being perfectly loved, of no longer fearing, no longer judging, no longer proving, no longer trying to earn God's attention and regard. For instance, what might we say instead of the ready quips colleagues find so amusing that ever so politely disparage another colleague's preaching? ("Well, she has her gifts, but preaching isn't one of them!") To what do we pay attention when we're not waiting for recognition to dawn on a new colleague's face upon realizing we're *that* cardinal rector? After a shift of heart, mind, attitude, or perception, we have to learn new matching behaviors of humility, kindness, and gentle speech, all of which takes time, attentive practice, and still more grace.

The advantage to us as preachers, then, is we can empathize with our colleagues and parishioners, and that gives us a deep understanding to use in our sermons. If there's a certain rate at which we accept our freedom as 100 percent loved, then there's a certain rate for everyone else too. They are learning at their own pace just as we are. Sometimes that pace is maddeningly slow for our petulant "Inner Jonahs" and our agendas, timelines, and wish lists for them. But, really, that just provides more fodder for empathy because they also have their "Inner Jonahs" about *us*, and they wish we'd hurry up too. But we can't hurry the process any more than they can. None of us can outpace the rate of grace.

If this were easy to believe, we would already: You are loved. You are loved. *You are loved.* "I believe, Lord. Help thou my unbelief."

## Preaching

*"Physician, heal thyself" (Luke 4:23; King James Version).*

The following may seem to be out of place to bring up this early in the book, because it may appear I'm advocating for mediocre sermons. That's not the case. Skill development for effective preaching is necessary for the best propagation of the Gospel. That's my mission and I hope it's yours. *And*, there are times when, to borrow my husband's term, we get "life'd."

There are many aspects of life and ministry beyond our control: people in the congregation die; the church basement floods; you're the solo pastor called for jury duty during Holy Week (yes, it happened to me, and no, I couldn't get out of it); or a crisis in town demands swift, prophetic action. And sometimes, our physical or mental health decides to take a nosedive without first consulting the preaching rota.

There are plenty of times we're called upon to preach "off-balance."[1] We can choose to gut out those days and try to preach the perfect sermon anyway. However, that's not necessarily a loving response to the reality of our limited time, energy, and emotional capacity. On

---

1. Thanks to the Rev'd Cathie Caimano for this phrase.

those days, I encourage you to do some personal pastoral care. Ask yourself what you would counsel a parishioner to do under similar circumstances. If you would offer a modicum of compassion about taking care of themselves, then the following will help you discern how to take care of yourself. First we need to ask ourselves whether we should preach at all. And second, if the answer is yes, then consider the "good enough" sermon.

### *Discern:* **Should *You Preach?***

To preach or not to preach? Occasionally, that *is* the question.

One of my seminary preaching students, Andrew, gave me permission to share his story. Andrew's wife gave birth to a baby boy, Nolan, three weeks early. There were many complications with the baby's development, and tragically, Nolan developed an infection and passed away at seventeen days old.

A couple of months later, Andrew was serving as the lector for Morning Prayer. The Hebrew Testament reading was the Judgment of Solomon, which tells the story of a baby who died. Andrew had read the lesson in advance and felt he was up to reading at chapel. He had to read the hard stuff sometime, he felt.

At the lectern, he opened the Bible and began to read. When the climax unfolded Andrew froze, unable to continue. Everyone in chapel froze with him. After a long pause, another member of the altar party walked to the lectern, gently put his hands on Andrew's shoulders to let him know he did not have to read, and finished for him.

Afterward, Andrew questioned his decision. *Did* he, in fact, have to read the hard stuff sometime? Did he have to confront the hard stuff *now*? What is the purpose of community when one is struggling, anyway? To ask someone to take his place would have been an honor. Andrew would have felt so if the situation were reversed, so why did he feel he needed to be tough and brave? Who would judge him for being affected by the passage, for the lesson to be too raw? How did reading serve him or the proclamation of God's Word?

These questions can be summarized by asking ourselves whether we are able to be in service to the Gospel when we're in the middle of extraordinary difficulties. Most of the time we can and do. We manage to preach during most of our physical, emotional, and spiritual trials. But there are times when we are overwhelmed. Sometimes we cannot contain our trials enough not to draw attention to ourselves and away from the Gospel, or we can't preach without causing ourselves further harm. When this happens, some preachers are blessed with colleagues who can take over, but most do not have this luxury. Particularly for them, a "Preaching Insurance Plan" for unexpected circumstances is worthwhile.

A Preaching Insurance Plan is the list of preaching resources at your disposal so you don't have to generate them under stress. For instance, are there retired clergy in your area? Could a layperson preach or a religious sister give a talk? Could you call a preaching buddy and swap pulpits? Is there a preacher on staff of another congregation who would like additional opportunities to preach? Is this the day for an ecumenical sermon and a preacher from another denomination? And don't you *need* another stewardship sermon from someone in the congregation? After all, stewardship is (truly) best accomplished with year-round sermons. This might be the perfect Sunday for one so you can steer clear of emotional subject matter. What would you list in your Preaching Insurance Plan?

These ideas might work for one Sunday, and we can be grateful for them. But after you have your one Sunday (or two, if you're really lucky) of respite, and assuming you can't take a temporary leave of absence, then what? How do we preach off-balance?

### The Good Enough Sermon

First, breathe deeply and treat yourself at least as well as you tell your parishioners to treat themselves. Second, ask yourself this: Are you doing the best you can? Are you managing as best as you know how? If you *are* doing your best, then you're acting as the faithful steward of God's Word you promised you would be. No one can do more than that, not even you. So don't try. This is a blessed limitation, a gift so we don't have to try to be superhuman and not quite leap over that tall building with regret.

If you are doing the best you can, then what's a "good enough" sermon during those extra-tough weeks when you get "life'd"? A good enough sermon says, "God loves you." The sermon might proclaim an aspect of God's love, like grace, mercy, or forgiveness, but the only message necessary is to remind people they're loved. The sermon doesn't have to be fancy, or a certain length (regardless of tradition), or say anything clever. The homily just has to have "Good" news.

A good enough sermon still has a point and a purpose, however, so we don't inflict our ramblings on our listeners. The point and purpose are discerned through the Good News and Prayer statements (see chapter 8). Not only do these statements keep our sermon focused; they also reduce the preacher's stress because they define the parameters of our emotional safety zone—that is, the boundaries within which we're able to preach without getting too close to the cliff's edge of our emotions. When we're managing our own heightened emotions, our judgment can be impaired. We may not be able to find enough objectivity to maintain our fiduciary duty to preach for our listeners and not for ourselves. If you're not sure whether your sermon stays within your emotional safety zone, vet it with a preaching buddy or trusted parishioner.

So, a good enough sermon has a point and purpose and stays within your emotional safety zone, clarified with Good News and Prayer statements. Check.

A good enough sermon is also organized with a beginning, middle, and end. The beginning is the introduction, which might be extra short, only a brief story or a paragraph. Be blunt if needed; the introduction only has to be long enough to get into the subject.

The middle is the body of the sermon. Make your point. Again, be blunt if necessary. Describe, "God loves you."

The end tells them again that God loves them because "the Bible tells us so." That's it. That's all that's required for a good enough sermon.

As to specific ideas for a good enough sermon . . .

1. For those who preach weekday sermons, consider the Sunday sermon to be more like one of those, *a short homily*, rather than a full-blown "sermon." Hardly anyone complains about a sermon being too short.

2. You can offer a sermon that has more to do with the Creed, corporate confession, or another *aspect of the liturgy* but to which you can still tie the lessons. These may be emotionally easier to handle on off-balance Sundays.

3. Another option is a "popcorn" sermon, though it's called by many names, like a dialogue or call-and-response sermon. The

preacher offers an idea, a problem, or a proposition and seeks responses from the congregation. The sermon becomes a controlled conversation. To do this effectively, you still have to have your Good News, Prayer, and Vision statements, so you know where you want the sermon to land and it doesn't accidentally wander where only fools dare to tread. Have in mind how you're going to start and conclude, even if the conclusion changes on the fly.

Give the listeners the "rules" for the sermon to control the length of the whole sermon and individual contributions, as well as its direction and tone. For instance, you might say remarks can only be six words long to push people to be pithy (and to riff off of Hemingway's supposed six-word novel: "For sale: baby shoes. Never worn."). Some will stick to the word limit, but others will start with, "I can't put this into six words, but . . ." However you decide to limit the responses (By time? Each person gets to speak only once?), you need to consider how you're going to contain the dialogue for those who ramble, get too personal or emotional, or feel they finally found their chance to use the bully pulpit. Remember the purpose still is to proclaim Good News, so think about how you want to include your listeners to witness to Jesus Christ.

4. *Old sermons.* You know how the "right" way to do something is the *first* way you learned it? My first (and only) homiletics prof, a Dominican priest, set my standard. He ripped up every sermon he preached so he would not be tempted to use them again. Not only did that become my "right" way, but when I've tried to recycle a sermon I've never been successful—the times and I had changed. The exception I've made to this rule are my story sermons, because they're timeless and not specific to a congregation, time, or place. Yet I still need to have a rationale to justify a story sermon is appropriate to offer to *these* people at *this* time with whatever is going on in the world *now*.

That said, many clergy feel successful recycling sermons, especially those who have moved to a new congregation or work as supply clergy. They feel recycling is good stewardship of their time and the message is as valuable to one congregation as another. They refresh a pertinent message to current circumstances and do so with less effort than starting over. After all, good books are worth rereading and good songs are listened to countless times, so a good sermon might be worth repeating too.

All in all, a recycled sermon might be the perfect good enough sermon. To help you discern whether or not to repeat a sermon, think how you'd feel if a recycled sermon were recognized by a listener. Let your comfort level be your guide.

5. What may be glaring in its absence is the mention of using *a sermon off the internet* as a good enough option. (See chapter 5 about preaching authentically.) I'll only say here I'm opposed. *Utterly*. I would prefer the integrity of announcing three minutes' silence to reflect on the Gospel than pretending another preacher's words were our own.

But an honest, related option *might* be to find the perfect sermon to read in its entirety, receive the author's permission, and give due credit. I've come close a few times because the message and prose couldn't be improved upon. Is this a possibility in off-balance circumstances?

While it has honesty in its favor, your ability to *read* the sermon has to be taken into account. Reading aloud compellingly enough to keep people's attention is a high-level skill. No matter how passionate you may feel about the sermon, few of us are trained sufficiently in public speaking or theater to pull this off. Listening to someone read aloud who doesn't have the chops is boring; the congregation is likely to disengage almost immediately. If, however, you *do* have the chops, having a few great sermons tucked away in your Preacher's Insurance Plan could be a good option.

## Conclusion

"Preacher, preach to thyself." Prescription:

1. If you preach that God loves your listeners, then preach to yourself that you are equally as loved.

2. If you object or have "reasons" why God can't or doesn't love you, you're just plain wrong, because you *are* loved. Be gentle with yourself knowing you can't outpace the rate of grace. You'll learn you're loved more than you think you are as soon as you're able to accept it. To help the process along, consider making an appointment to see your spiritual director, confessor, and/or therapist.

3. If you trust you are loved by God, give thanks. Ask for that love to be deepened until you no longer live for yourself alone, but for Christ crucified.

4. Be your own pastor and give yourself the counsel you'd give your parishioners. If you can't preach or need to preach a good enough sermon, so what? God will love you neither more nor less for bumping up against your limits.

# CHAPTER FOUR

# Lectio for Sermons

### Good News

The Good News speaks for itself:
"This is the way. Walk in it" (Isa 30:21).

### Prayer

I pray you move in sheer silence to the entrance to the cave
when you hear God will pass by.

### Problem

Impatience to find the sermon message
blinds our eyes and stops our ears.

### Vision

We are renewed and come closer to God through sermon prep.

### Chapter in a Sentence

Trust God to reveal the message in due time.

### Latch

Slow is fast.

(The workbook to integrate this chapter with your backstory and preaching
can be found at www.backstorypreaching.com.)

## Backstory

*When Elijah heard [the sound of sheer silence], he wrapped his face in his mantle and went out and stood at the entrance of the cave (1 Kgs 19:13).*

You're driving on a road trip. The day is fine and the road dry, the sun is strong and the fields dried golden brown. You're on the interstate with clear roads, and traffic is sparse. The posted speed limit is 75 mph and you're taking it at 80. Cruise control is engaged, your favorite music playing, head swaying to the rhythm. The car needs gas, though. The next exit ramp has a posted limit of 25 mph with a sharp curve to the right. You turn off the cruise control, ease into the exit lane, and slow down. The car is at 50 when you begin the curve, which feels like crawling compared to 80, but that's not slow enough. You hit the brakes to slow down more, but the curve is so tight you feel yourself leaning to the left, tires gripping to keep you on the pavement. Just as you finish the curve and straighten out, you finally get down to 25, and you and the car settle in to safety.

*Whew!* Even though you've quickly slowed from a high speed on straight roads to a slow speed for a curve countless times, you're still surprised by the rapid transition. You're also surprised, because as an experienced driver, you *know* better . . . but *still* didn't slow down in a safe way. It takes another minute for your heart rate to return to normal and your body to recalibrate from the feeling of driving 80 to inching along at 25.

When we're speeding along in our ministries going 80, trying to notice a sermon message is like whizzing past that color purple in the field—a surprising, unmistakable blur of color against the monotony of yellow browns. And then it's gone. You're already past. You think about turning around but the next exit isn't for miles. Besides, it'll take too long to drive back and you didn't notice the mile marker. You're not sure you could even find it again, so you keep going at 80, hoping something else will hurry up and show itself. But you kick yourself a little, knowing that the purple in that field might have been exactly what you needed. You know if you'd been going slower you could have stopped in time.

Conversely, when our minds and spirits are inching along at 25, we're going slow enough to stop anytime we want. We can not only stop and look but walk into the middle of it, distinguish the purples from the indigos, touch the violets and inhale the lavenders. Then we can sit at eye level, ready and prepared to witness God's glory showing itself in an ombre of purples.

Elijah didn't drive speeding cars, but he did have a mind that surely raced as fast as ours. I imagine Elijah also needed to slow his mind from 80 to 25. He needed to slow his mind and still his spirit as he walked from the back of the cave to the front so he could be ready. Knowing he could miss it, Elijah prepared for God's glory to show itself in silent passage.

We need to prepare ourselves, too. We stand at the back of the cave multitasking, one eye scanning our lists, deadlines, and the clock, while the other scans the lessons, praying for a sermon message to show up ASAP. *Lectio divina* helps us slow down to be fully present to God as God passes by in silence. *Lectio divina* is a centuries-old process of holy reading that engages us in Scripture so that it forms us into itself: a holy word. It's a profound process that slowly draws us from the back of the cave to the front.

*Lectio divina* for sermon prep is paradoxical. Here's the beauty and surprise of this prayerful process: We engage slowly to write an authentic sermon more quickly. My Suzuki violin teacher used to say, "Playing fast is playing slow—just faster." She was referring to a practice technique to learn to play a piece of music up to tempo. The technique requires the musician to practice at a slow, relaxed tempo. If at any point the tempo feels too fast and the player tenses up, notes are garbled. Music isn't created. The tension is a clue that a section needs to be worked on. That section is practiced ever more slowly until it reaches its own slow, relaxed tempo. The speed is then increased one notch at a time until it's played as relaxed and "slowly" as the rest of the piece. Thus, a well-played, fast-tempo piece is played slowly, just faster.

For preachers, too, slow is fast. We need to slow down to engage Scripture and to be able to hear what God has to reveal to us. To slam into sermon prep at high speed with impatience or fear and anxiety over what we're going to say, stops our eyes from focusing and plugs our ears to the Spirit's whispers made in sheer silence. Fear keeps us in performance mode, moving at top speed, looking for a lighted billboard with the sermon message blinking on it. *Lectio divina* shifts us from 80 to 25. *Shhhhh . . .* Be quiet. Be still. Breathe. Relax. Listen to the Spirit's whispers, feel the gentle nudges to bring us to the front of the cave, ready when God passes by. Don't *do* anything. Don't fret. The sermon message will reveal itself. Gentle down, sink deep, and let the Spirit's currents bring the message to us.

*Slow is fast.*

To make slow fast, we need to prepare ourselves to wait at the entrance to the cave, ready for God to reveal the sermon's message. This takes courage to trust God is in the process and will offer a message our people need to hear. Courage is needed also to trust that sermons are found more in breathing and emptiness, and in the quiet drowsiness upon waking from a night's rest, than in rooting out a message as if we were a terrier scrabbling after a badger.

What does it take for *you* to slow down to be able to listen? What do you have to do to be alone with God and wait silently, trusting? What do you need to do to be able to rest in a field of purple? What do you need to slow down from 80 to 25?

### A Sermon Prep Ritual

When you move into the exit lane on the highway, you employ a necessary plan no matter how much of a hurry you're in. This plan has become so automatic and works so well you probably don't think about it, and yet each step is vital to bring you to your destination: look in the rearview mirror, engage the turn signal, check for blind spots, rotate the steering wheel, depress the brake pedal, and keep your eyes on the road. After years of practice these steps flow unconsciously to bring you dependably to your journey's end.

Our journey's end for sermon prep is the front of the cave, but hurrying forward from the back leaves us breathless, with scattered thoughts and anxious heart. But God deserves our undivided attention. We need a plan to transition us gently from the crush of daily concerns to quiet listening. A sermon prep ritual re-collects us physically, mentally, and spiritually so we are prepared for God with singleness of body, mind, and spirit. Physically, we offer up to God the time of day we do our best work, and prepare the location and our bodies. Mentally, we prepare to focus and set aside the distractions. Spiritually, we ready ourselves to say "yes" to God's word.

First, make plans for your body, beginning with the time of day. We offer to God as a spiritual sacrifice the time of day we are best able to be still and listen to the Spirit. When is that time of day for you? Is it first thing when the drowsiness of sleep has not quite fled for the day and the to-do lists are yet to hold you in their thrall? Perhaps it's in the still, quiet coziness of late night when you feel like you have the whole world to yourself. Or maybe it's midday when you feel freed up after taking care of the day's most pressing demands? What part of the day are you best able to give your whole self to God's word?

The location is important, too. The location creates an environment most conducive to encountering the Spirit. Prepare that space as thoughtfully as preparing for liturgy. Moreover, just as different liturgies have different requirements, there are different requirements for the stages of sermon prep. *Lectio*, for instance, might best be done with your favorite Bible in a quiet corner, in silence, with an icon and lighted candle. During *meditatio* (chapter 6), we conduct research. We need resources like books, the internet, and yellow pads. Where do you have best access to these materials? It might be your home or church office, or the local library. *Oratio* (chapter 8) is the outpouring. Where do you feel most free to let the Spirit move through you? Maybe it's at the local coffee shop where you're inspired by others who are as absorbed in their writing as you are. Or it might be taking your laptop and notes to the park where you are inspired by flowers on the ground, clouds in the sky, and God's infinite universe that touches the crown of your head. Where does God call you to do each stage of this holy work and prepare it with care and reverence?

What about your body itself? What does it need to be quiet and still? Possibilities include yoga, stretching, vigorous exercise, or a nap. Bring in your five senses, too. What clothes should touch you to make you feel relaxed yet alert? Sweats or clergy shirt with collar? How about a soft blanket on your lap? What do you wish to taste? Coffee, tea, ice water with lemon? How about sight and smell? I combine these by making a habit of maintaining fresh flowers on my desk; it never ceases to surprise me how much this simple practice makes me smile with gratitude and wonder while I work. You might also include essential oils, burning incense, inspiring artwork, candles or icons, and have a beautiful landscape or cityscape out the windows. While you work, what do you hear? From silence, to music, to a gentle wind, to computer apps designed to enhance mental focus, what will help you listen most keenly for the Spirit?

Put the physical preparation together and we have a plan to offer God our bodies, our best time of day, and the most conducive environment for this sacred work. It may take time to prepare but that preparation is not time spent away from work as if we were sloughing off; it's time spent for our best, most efficient work to listen to and speak the word of God. What do you need to transition yourself and move from the back of the cave to the front?

We also need to prepare ourselves mentally so we are single-minded, ready to wait on God alone. We need to let go of distracting thoughts. Every thought vies for our attention, and each time we follow one it takes that much more time and effort to return our gaze to that empty space in front of the cave. The solution for this is a simple one: a brain dump.

A brain dump is a repository of thoughts, lists, and worries. It's a secure space to capture anything in our heads that lures our attention away from the task at hand. Getting our thoughts out of our heads keeps us more in the present instead of ruminating on the past, and more frequently, planning for the future. We scribble our thoughts and lists so they no longer compete for our attention.

The repository of a brain dump might be a simple piece of paper and a pen to scribble our to-do lists, or a calendar to record our lists in a more organized fashion. The repository might also include a journal. A journal to hold our worries and worst-case scenarios can help us let go of these thoughts. They help us see how ridiculous they (usually) are. Record in a journal, for example, the worst-case scenario if a sermon doesn't come together, or you can't figure out the perfect ending, or a listener falls asleep from boredom. Ego and pride are bruised, but beyond that, what's the worst thing that could happen? God will banish you to the outer darkness with the wailers and teeth gnashers? Once we spin out our worst nightmares, we can usually see our fears are not only unlikely, but laughable. A brain dump empties the thoughts from our heads, both the practical and fearsome ones. Once unloaded our heads are ready to be filled with thoughts of God, and God alone. What ritual would help you be single-minded?

So, we have considered plans for body and mind, and now we consider our spirit. Our spiritual preparation for sermon work is the most important because we have a choice to make every time we prepare for sermon prep: We can either be drained dry by the external demands created by preaching's relentless and implacable deadlines, or surprisingly, be filled by them.

We are asked weekly by our communities to step away from other demands, dig deep into Scripture, be astonished by the divine graciousness we find there, and then share what was revealed. Stop for a moment and ponder the gift of this. If we condoned lotteries, we could claim we had won the vocational jackpot because spiritual respite is our vocation! Respite means to be relieved from our usual responsibilities in order to be renewed. When we step away from ministry's daily responsibilities, prepare ourselves body, mind, and spirit to steep in God's presence, we are renewed. Because preaching is relentless, we get to dig into Scripture every week. And because the deadlines are implacable, we get to move regularly away from other duties to stand at the entrance to the cave. We get to turn our attention toward that empty chasm outside the cave knowing God will pass by, and that we will be the first to see the divine on behalf of our communities. We are asked to see, and hear, and touch, and taste what the Lord has done and bring that knowledge back to those who wait for it. Seriously, what's better than being *asked* to spend our time being filled with the presence of God? What's a better way to use our days, weeks, and years, world without end? Indeed, our vocation to preach offers us perpetual spiritual respite. We are most blessed among vocations!

So how do you need to prepare your spirit for respite? The steps might include personal *lectio divina*, contemplative prayer, praying the rosary, singing Taizé chants, listening to music, journaling, and/or artwork. What will bring your spirit into alignment with God's purposes for your time together to revel and grow in the Word?

Set aside thirty minutes now to create your sermon prep ritual. Because it takes several weeks for new practices to become habitual and most new practices feel awkward and uncomfortable, follow it for six weeks. Don't second-guess yourself or alter it until the trial ends; then evaluate and make changes. If you want a suggestion you can look at my ritual to prepare for *lectio* at the end of this chapter. Take the time to discern and follow your plan to enter into spiritual respite step by step until it's automatic, and wallow in your time alone with God.

## Preaching

*"This is the way; walk in it" (Isa 30:21).*

We often feel that the hardest part of sermon prep is to discover the message or the writing. But ironically, for many preachers the hardest part is actually the first and simplest thing we do: read the text. The first stage of *lectio divina* is *lectio*, "to read." *Lectio* is hard for many of us because it requires us to let the text *be*.

*Lectio divina* requires us to be humble and vulnerable to the text. By its very nature, *lectio divina* integrates spirituality into sermon preparation. When we let the text be we practice humility and vulnerability. Brené Brown defines vulnerability as "uncertainty, risk, and emotional exposure."[1] Praying *lectio* is uncertain because we encounter God, and who knows how God will make the most of our undivided attention? It's risky because we can't know what direction the Scriptures might take us, the human sinfulness it might reveal, or the emotions it might expose. Scripture mirrors our wounds, disappointments, frustrations, doubts, jealousies, betrayals, and, perhaps, the most vulnerable emotion of all, hope. Scripture is the Word of God, and it will speak to us what we need to hear. Not knowing what's coming humbles and makes us vulnerable, indeed.

*Lectio* requires us to let Scripture be an entity unto itself. We respect Scripture as the means of revelation, as a vehicle that divulges God's glory. When we respect Scripture as its own "being," we honor it. We don't presume to manipulate God's Word or impose our desire or will upon it. We don't use the Word as a means to an end—assuaging our anxiety and providing us with a sermon message. *Lectio* grows holy fear and awe to be in the presence of the Lord and the countless people who were vulnerable enough to say yes to God's will. Because they said "yes," they still teach us . . . *if* we let ourselves be vulnerable enough to be taught.

Consider Scripture this way: While God always cares about us and speaks to us through Scripture, there's also a way in which Scripture is indifferent to us. The people in Scripture will live, continue on, and fill the world with God's goodness whether or not we ever read a

---

1. Brené Brown, *Daring Greatly: How the Courage to Be Vulnerable Transforms the Way We Live, Love, Parent, and Lead* (New York: Gotham, 2012), 2.

word. Those in Scripture don't *need* us. Scripture's lack of dependence on us lets us offer our respect and dignify its people accordingly.

This attitude allows us to enjoy God's writings without asking anything of those described. We can see the characters as their own people who lived without ever knowing we would read about them one day. When they lived, we were of no consideration to them. As a result, we can approach them as human beings independent from us with their own stories, their own concerns, cares, and worries, their own families, their own mixed motivations, and their own ups and downs with God. The people in the Bible did not exist to provide us with sermon fodder. They existed because God made them. They deserve for us to treat them with all the dignity with which God ennobled them.

This is true not only for the characters in the Bible, but also for Scripture settings, geography, poetry, prophecies, and plot lines. When we pray *lectio*, we are *guests* in their world. We have been invited into that world by God who nudged scribes to record their stories. A *lectio* mind lets us see the worlds contained in the Bible as we do when we explore any new culture, with their own innate integrity—their own languages, foods, architecture, vocations, habits, and family norms.

When we feel the anxiety of the sermon deadline, we can easily presume upon the Bible's culture as if the people there exist only to get us out of a jam and give us a message for our congregation. Instead, *lectio* lets us encounter Scripture not as our problem to be solved, but as an unfolding, a wondering, a chance to get curious about these people, anticipate discovery, and be altered in the process.

So we start with the hardest place: *To let Scripture be*. To see it *as it is*, word for word, phrase by phrase, person by person, as literally as "literal" means. To regard something in its own integrity is to honor the Creator who made it. "All things came into being with him, and without him, not one thing came into being" (John 1:3). God created all things through Jesus Christ because God wanted to. When we see something as it is, we admire the Creator and the Creator's imagination and artistry, and so, we "praise" God. What a gift to have a vocation in which part of the job is to appreciate, gasp, laugh, and puzzle over this great universe God invented!

*Lectio* slows us down to hear, touch, taste, smell, and intuit what is in the text. When we use our senses, we remember there's much of human experience that never changes. The odor of unwashed bodies, the plop of a donkey's hooves on a dirt road, the taste of sea salt, the cacophony of a market crowd, the distance a voice travels across calm water, the fear of being chased, the shame of being insulted or ignored. *Lectio* guides us to be *in* Scripture.

To pray *lectio*, read the passage several times. Read out loud. Read in different tones of voice. Read with an accent. Read as a child who wouldn't understand half the words. Take note of who is in the story, where it happens, the time, the season, the objects mentioned, the materials, and the buildings. In your imagination stand still and turn around 360 degrees. What do you see, hear, smell, taste, and feel? Pastorally, what do you sense? Danger, discord, joy, frustration, surprise? Notice the *exact* sequence of events. We're so familiar with the story, we think we know how it goes. We forget that the order in which people speak, how they speak, and to whom matters.

Pay attention especially to things that don't make sense. Where are the glitches? For example, when the widow put her widow's mite in the Temple treasury box, Jesus was across the street. How could he see how much she put in the box? How will she eat and where will she live now that she's given "all she has"? Jesus doesn't offer to help with her immediate needs; why not? Another example: Bartimaeus was obviously blind. The most likely thing Bartimaeus would ask was to see again, yet Jesus asks Bartimaeus what he *wants*. Why did Jesus ask? Sometimes what makes us curious is what's *not* said. The Epistles, for instance, usually address problems in fledgling Christian communities. If Paul felt he needed to tell the Corinthians that love is patient and kind, then it's likely the Corinthians were acting *im*patient and *un*kind. Why?

Another way to engage *lectio* is to act as a stage director sitting in the theater. Write the script and include the characters' tones of voices. Block their movements, and hand them their costumes and props. Sit in the seats and let the rehearsal run; then mix it up and try it another way.

Alternatively, write the lesson in your own words. Write the text as if you were writing to someone who had never heard the story before. Or, rewrite the story as a series of limericks or memes, or draw it out as a series of stick figures and speech bubbles.

Now that I've given some suggestion to pray *lectio* for sermon prep, let me return to the reason *lectio* is so hard for preachers. During lec-tio, *you don't get to make meaning.* During *lectio* you don't get to jump to conclusions; you don't get to wonder where the sermon message is; you don't get to ponder what you'll preach. We're so practiced at looking for messages, it's extremely difficult to set aside the hunt for "Ooh, that'll preach!" That part is coming, I promise. But during *lectio* we are tuning in to the sound of sheer silence. We are touching and noticing the color, texture, and patterns in the cave walls as we move toward the entrance to wait for God, but we're not standing in the entrance yet. Have patience, trust, let yourself be vulnerable to the text without interference. Set aside your education, assumptions, presumptions, and impatience for a message.

Trust God. Trust Scripture. Slow is fast.

## Conclusion

To discern a sermon that transforms both preacher and listener re-quires the preacher to model that vulnerability from the moment we approach the text. We model vulnerability in the process of sermon prep when we say yes to God's will as it is revealed in these words. We start our sermon prep with *lectio* by approaching the text in hu-mility, without presumption, and with respect to let God's Word be as it is, just as it has been handed down to us.

Trust in God's mercy, grace, and will. Never forget that God wants the Gospel to be shared more than we do. God will reveal the mes-sage that needs to be revealed and, in the process, re-form us to be the Word we preach.

Guide to *Lectio* for Sermon Prep

1. Prepare yourself with your sermon prep ritual.

2. Read the text out loud.

3. Read the text out loud again, and record it into your smartphone or another device. Listen to the recording each day, while you drive, exercise, walk the dog, and/or before you go to sleep.

4. Pause.

5. Read the text again, perhaps in a different tone of voice so you hear it another way. Jot down notes of any "glitches," questions, or "gaps" you see or have about the text. What is making you curious?

6. Pause.

7. Read the text again.

   Choose one or more of these, or a process of your own design. Do the following with all the texts, one of them, or the portions of the texts that most intrigue you:

   • Map out the scene(s) as if you were a stage director.
   • Draw the text in comic book fashion.
   • Rewrite the text in your own words.
   • Draw or write on a copy of the text the words and phrases that stand out.

8. *Contemplatio.*

   • Rest in the texts in silence. Let the texts be.
   • Pray before you go to sleep. Ask God to recreate you into the Word you speak.
   • Have a way to record thoughts that arise as you wake.

   *Example: My Sermon Prep Ritual for the First Stage of* Lectio

Body. First thing in the morning. Stretch. Pajamas or loose clothes. Make coffee or tea. Have an icon and my Bible. Sit in my backyard whenever possible, or my easy chair. Essential oils. Turn off all phone notifications. Listen to birds or my music concentration app.

Mind. Do a brain dump in my calendar. Keep it handy to record thoughts when they arise.

Spirit. Listen to Bible daily readings app. Conscious breathing, then contemplative prayer.

(For more practical suggestions, the workbook to integrate this chapter with your backstory and preaching can be found at www.backstorypreaching.com.)

# CHAPTER FIVE

# The One and Only

### Good News

The Good News is there is only one of you,
and you were asked to preach.

### Prayer

I pray you see that your incarnation of the Gospel
is necessary and sufficient.

### Problem

Doubt prevents us from trusting we have enough to offer.

### Vision

Listeners receive your wholehearted incarnation of the Gospel
as only you can offer it.

### Chapter in a Sentence

You're the one and only person who can preach your sermon;
don't deprive us of that gift.

### Latch

A story

(The workbook to integrate this chapter with your backstory and preaching
can be found at www.backstorypreaching.com.)

## Backstory

*"You did not choose me but I chose you. And I appointed you to go and bear fruit"* (John 15:16).

"Authenticity" is a buzz word right now.

Apparently, "authentic" has lost a bit of its meaning due to its overuse in the culture. It's too bad because it's a terribly important word and I won't apologize for its use. Preachers need to speak the truth, the small piece of the larger Truth that each of us knows. We need to speak the truth that has come to us and is given to us to share, as only each of us could know it. We need to speak the Truth that is authentic to us.

At a diocesan clergy conference, a retired priest who still has the opportunity to preach regularly, approached me and said, "I want to apply for your Backstory Preaching Mentorship program, but I'm not sure I can. I've lost my voice."

I wasn't sure what she meant by that. "Physically, or spiritually?" I asked her. With a pained expression, she said it was the latter. She told me she didn't feel she belonged in the pulpit. She said she wasn't qualified, that her preaching training hadn't been enough. She felt she didn't know enough. She truly believed she shouldn't be preaching.

She went on to tell me about her ministry. Some years prior she was in a small plane accident with four other people. Not knowing whether they would live or die, for seventeen minutes the plane circled over the Gulf of Mexico. As they descended ever closer to the water, the pilot searched for a boat close enough to come to their rescue . . . if they survived.

The priest told me that during those seventeen minutes she experienced the exquisite love of God. Nothing but the love of God. In spite of the imminent possibility of dying, she felt the peace of God that passes all understanding. In fact, she experienced so much love and peace, she knew with absolute certainty that her daughter, a senior in high school, would be OK, too, whichever way the landing went. In those seventeen minutes, she said, she knew the love of God.

She looked at me and added, "I *know* the love of God." Impassioned, she went on to say that ever since then, her ministry has been *love*. With tears in her eyes, she told me she wants *everyone* to know the love of God.

I looked straight at her and said, "*That* is what qualifies you to preach." She was stunned. For a moment, speechless. "You mean, it's not the books?" she asked.

"No, it's not the books. Books are great. They answer questions. But what people need to hear is about the love of God. That it's real. And you can tell them. Because you know." Slowly, she nodded. "Yes, I *know*."

There was a long pause as she caught her breath. Then she asked, "So with your process, what would you do with, say, the Good Samaritan?" I responded, "What would *you* do with the Good Samaritan?" In ten minutes I walked her through the process. Traveling through *lectio*, *meditatio*, *oratio*, and *contemplatio*, I asked her questions. Lightbulbs kept turning on. At the end she was able to name, succinctly and clearly, the Good News. The Good News would be the message for a beautiful sermon: "Always choose Love." She concluded, "I found my voice."

This priest gave me permission to share her story. She reminds me of the Samaritan woman at the well who discovers Jesus during the course of a conversation, so I'm going to call her "Sam." Sam discovered Jesus was already within her, because Jesus' love was already within her. Knowing his love for her and everyone is the most important message she could give to any listener.

Imagine Sam's congregation. Imagine the gift to them to hear from someone like her, someone who can speak intimately and passionately about what they most want and need to hear because Sam knows it for herself. And because Sam knows it for herself, she knows it is true for them just as much.

Now imagine those who have never heard that God loves them. How palpable is the *absence* of that knowledge though they don't know what's missing, as if a hole precedes their every step. They sense the hole as an out-of-focus pit they're always dodging. How sad for those who never realize that awareness of God's love for them will fill the pit and they can walk unguardedly! And who better to tell them than Sam, because Sam is uniquely qualified to tell people that God loves them with all God is and ever will be.

Sam is uniquely qualified not only because of her incident on the plane, though. She is uniquely qualified because of all she is and all that made her who she is. Sam is the only one in the history and entirety of creation to have been made in her particularity of God's image,[1] born into her specific family, to have received her experiences of teachers, playmates, siblings, church attendance, and school. She's the only one who took those people and experiences into her exact clergy training to sift Scripture, tradition, and reason through her being. And then, she is the only one to bring all of herself, all of her education, and all of the church's authority to preach to her congregation. Literally, *only she* can share with them *in her way* what she knows *uniquely*: "Always choose Love." Multiply the odds that her stories would cross with the unique stories of each listener, and this infinitesimally small number makes my head hurt! How sad would it be, then, were she not to share with them what God has revealed to and through her alone?

We have some really great preachers in the world, thanks be to God. Perhaps there's a preacher you particularly admire. Perhaps there are times you wished you preached like they do. But I don't wish that. We have one of them already. We don't need another one.

We need you.

You're the only one who knows God in the way you do, the only one who can reveal God to us in the way you can. If you don't tell us, we'll never know. Please, don't deprive us.

### Preaching Is Your Life . . . Your Life Is Preaching

We all have kids in our lives. Parish kids, our own kids, neighbors, nieces and nephews. One of the hard things about being a grown-up is to understand we're always teaching kids something. The only question is, *what* are we teaching?

---

1. A fun factoid—the number of atoms in the average human male is "$10^{27}$." But the odds that any one person made it to existence? 1 in $10^{2,685,000}$. That's a 10 followed by 2,685,000 zeroes. "So what's the probability of your existing? It's the probability of 2 million people getting together—about the population of San Diego—each to play a game of dice with *trillion-sided dice.* They each roll the dice, and they all come up the exact same number—say, 550,343,279,001." Ali Binazir, "What Are the Chances of Your Coming into Being?," *Meanderings over Heaven, Earth, and Mind* (blog), June 15, 2011, http://blogs.harvard.edu/abinazir /2011/06/15/what-are-chances-you-would-be-born/.

If we speak respectfully, we're teaching respectful behavior. If we hug them when they skin a knee or feel disappointed about a grade, we're teaching empathy and compassion. If we yell at them when they accidentally break our favorite coffee mug, we're teaching the value of things and anger. If we then apologize for our outburst, we're teaching humility and forgiveness.

There's nothing we do that doesn't teach kids something. The food we eat. The exercise we get. Our behavior in heavy traffic. The movies we watch and books we read. The prayers we say and money we spend. Without a moment's exception, we're teaching what we believe living as a child of God means.

Being a preacher puts us in the same position. Our life is *preaching.* The only question is, *what* are we preaching?

Everything we do and say displays what we believe living as a child of God means. Every choice we make reveals what we believe about God and where our face is turned. Are we facing toward God or away? Are we loving God above all other loves, and are we loving our neighbor as ourselves? Or not so much?

As church leaders, we need to know that people are always watching us, taking cues from us, measuring us against explicit and implicit standards they think befit preachers. We can't do anything about people's standards, expectations, or perceptions. But that doesn't mean we're not still sending messages about the Gospel in word and deed, with things done and left undone. We have to decide the ways we want to live that are as congruent as possible with the Good News. We have to decide how to live so we are always preaching Good News, in thought, word, and deed, with what we do and what we leave undone.

As preachers, we accepted a call to preach always. I recall a famous basketball player whose behavior was not always exemplary. When questioned about the impact his choices might be having on young people, his retort was that he was paid to play basketball, not to be a role model. No, he wasn't paid to be a role model and yet the truth was that he was a role model whether he wanted to be or not. We're in a similar position. We preach all the time, whether we want to or not. Some of us may feel uncomfortable, or even resentful, that our job as Christian preachers never ceases, that it's our job and vocation to preach the Gospel at *all* times and in *all* places. You're right; we never get a day off. But we don't get a "day off" because we're called to *preach*, but because our *baptisms* first established our 24/365 vocation.

Prior to being ordained, we were baptized. Our baptisms are what started us on the path to preach at all times and places. Whether we're ordained or not, to be Christian is to preach always. (My liturgics professor used to say that our baptismal certificates ought to be the size of our ordination certificates and vice versa. How many of us have on our office walls a huge baptismal certificate, framed and hanging above our degrees and certificates of ordination?) The ministry of the baptized is to preach the Gospel with our lives. And yes, as the ordained, we're modeling for others what that looks like. We're modeling every time we speak and the way we act toward the pleasant parishioners and the unpleasant, toward our lay leaders and staff, toward the homeless and hungry, toward our family, the Earth, and . . . *hear this* . . . ourselves. People take their cues from us, and we are scrutinized and held to a higher standard, whether we want to be or not. We are always modeling and preaching *something* about God. The question is, what is it?

For our sermons' messages to be authentic and trustworthy, they have to be the same messages we preach *out* of the pulpit. No matter where it's preached, the messages we offer are shaped by our entire lives. Everything we are goes with us into the pulpit. There is no part of ourselves left out. Our whole person, our whole being, preaches. The Scriptures run through our childhoods, preaching formation, and the experience of our ministry context to uncover the message our listeners most need to hear.

Using the worksheet and labyrinth that follow, we can reflect on what makes each of us uniquely formed to preach as only each of us can.[2]

In the left labyrinth we have our "Human Becoming." This includes our families of origin, where we grew up, our education, experiences of church and church leaders, Enneagram orientation, prayer practices, and early encounters with God. Our current prayer practices and acquaintance with Scripture are here as they continue to shape us. Use the worksheet to reflect, then write on the ingoing path those aspects that formed us and take us deep into the quiet center of God. *We are wondrously and marvelously made!* After staying

---

2. An easier-to-use, full-page image for you to fill in is included in the accompanying workbook. Find it at www.backstorypreaching.com.

## Instructions to Prepare for the Labyrinth

Our whole lives preach. Everything we are and everything we've done comes with us into the pulpit. Prayerfully consider the many parts of your life that enter your sermons. Use the suggestions below to reflect and take notes.

Next, select the most important of these to write on the "ingoing" path of each circle. Leave the center and "outgoing" path blank. "Walk out" in holy silence to enter the next labyrinth.

The center of the triple labyrinth represents where the Word of God resides in you. Combined with preparation for each sermon, this is the birthplace of your sermons. Rest here in contemplation.

When you are ready, retrace your steps. Walk past in silence and gratitude. When you exit the labyrinth your sermon is within you, ready to be written and offered.

| *Examples of Human Becoming* | *Examples of Preaching Formation* | *Examples of Preaching Context* |
|---|---|---|
| Family of origin | Training | Demographics |
| Places you lived | Professors | Location |
| Schools | Mentors | Economic |
| Pets | Favorite | influences |
| Friends | preachers | Political |
| Church | Favorite sermons | leanings |
| Health | Cont. Education | Local traditions |
| | Influential books | Biblical literacy |
| | | Languages |

## Preaching is Your Life; Your Life is Preaching

*Fill in the "ingoing" path; leave the "outgoing" path in silence.*

Calligraphy & Design Laura R. Norton, www.lettersaloft.com.    © Lisa Cressman, 2016. Used with permission.
©Lisa Cressman, 2018

in the center to acknowledge and thank God for all that shaped us (the joyful, the heartbreaking, the fun, the harmful, and the happy and unhappy surprises), we circle back past them all in silence and continue into the top labyrinth.

The top labyrinth is our "Preaching Formation." This is our formal and informal education where we learned to preach. You can reflect on the ingoing path about your call to ordained ministry, the setting in which and subjects you studied, teachers, clinical pastoral education, field education, mentors, and the states of the world and church. Again, in the center we acknowledge to God everything these gave us (the joyful, the heartbreaking, the fun, the harmful, and the happy and unhappy surprises). In silence we circle back past them all and continue to the right labyrinth.

In this labyrinth we consider our "Ministry Context," the setting where we are called to preach. It includes our ordination, church tradition, and the authority given to us to enter the pulpit, plus those we serve in the congregation and community, and our pastoral relationships. It also includes social justice, corporate worship, and our attitudes and practices of our sermon prep. Write on the ingoing path what is most significant for you. Then again, in the center we acknowledge to God all we know that forms us as preachers (the joyful, the heartbreaking, the fun, the harmful, and the happy and unhappy surprises), and circle back past them all in silence.

The right labyrinth empties into the very center where, waiting to meet us, is the Word of God. The Word of God is shaped in us through all that's within these three sacred circles and more we cannot name. The Word can't be shaped or formed in any other fashion other than by working through the unique configuration that makes us who we are. No one else can preach the same sermon because no one else has lived or been formed as we have.

The Word of God is formed in this holy center of our beings. When we enter this space of discernment, we are creating with God akin to Michelangelo's understanding of his task as a sculptor: "The best artist has that thought alone which is contained within the marble shell; the sculptor's hand can only break the spell to free the figures slumbering in the stone."[3] As preachers, each of us alone has a mes-

---

3. "Michelangelo quotes," BrainyQuote, http://www.brainyquote.com/quotes/quotes/m/michelange402372.html.

sage of Good News that God forms within us. Through our sermon preparation, the Holy Spirit releases the message to bless all who hear it.

It's in this heart of hearts, the center and core of our beings, where we discern the sermon's message. While our sermon prep includes responsible and sufficient study, an authentic message doesn't come from books or someone else's words. An authentic message comes from being formed by God through our entire lives. A genuine sermon comes from being so overwhelmed by God's love that we can't wait to tell others they are loved just as much.

I invite you now to fill in your labyrinth. Alter the suggestions to suit.

## Preaching

*"What is truth?" (John 18:38).*

The backstory of your life and spirituality integrate with the craft of preaching when you accept that there is no one else who can preach like you, that your preaching is necessary, and that your authentic self is sufficient. That is, you don't have to add anyone extra.

The *Apple Dictionary* cites the root of "authentic" as coming from Greek, *"authentikos,* 'principal, genuine.'" The root of "genuine," is "from the Latin, *genuinus,* from *genu,* 'knee,'" which references the Roman custom of a father acknowledging his paternity of a newborn child by placing the baby on his knee.

Your message is genuine from you. It's born from your DNA and bears the unmistakable mark of your paternity/maternity. No one would mistake your sermon for someone else's because it was formed in the intersection of your life and the unique imprint of God in you. The only vehicle you have available to birth a sermon is through you. When you believe the Good News you preach, it is by definition an authentic sermon.

We offer an authentic sermon of Good News in hopes that our listeners will also believe, but we can only hope they will. The theme of the Good News is we are loved and forgiven in perfect freedom. We are all free to choose the love of God or turn Love down. We are free to accept God's mercy or reject it. We are utterly, perfectly, eternally free to accept the Gospel, return the Good News to its owner, or pretend Love never existed. So, if we are going to be not only authentic preachers but authentic witnesses of Jesus Christ, the only way we can offer the Good News is in perfect freedom. Listeners can choose to accept the invitation to believe or not.

That means with every quotation, anecdote, poem, and word choice, our homiletical, ethical questions are these: Do our words say "God loves you," and "God forgives you"? And are they said in such a way that listeners are welcome to accept or ignore the invitation to believe? If we're not saying "God loves and forgives you," and we're not making that declaration in perfect freedom, then we're using words to achieve some other goal. We're using words as tools to manipulate our listeners for some other end, usually our own.

To "manipulate" simply means to handle or control something skillfully, like manipulating a knife to mince herbs, or manipulating a race car through a tight scrum on the track's curve. We also manipulate words. When we preach, we hope to manipulate our words skillfully so our message is clearly understood. However, there's another meaning of manipulation that isn't so honorable. Turning to the *Apple Dictionary* again, it defines manipulation as, "To control or influence cleverly, unfairly, or unscrupulously, e.g., to alter or present so as to mislead."

For most of us, the misleading type of preaching manipulation is rarely done on purpose, but we are human beings who are not pure of heart, but of mixed motivation. Some of our motives serve God's purposes, some serve others', and some serve our own. We often don't recognize in the moment when we're attempting to mislead, but we need to discern our hearts. To help us discern, here is a preacher's "*examen* of conscience."

1. *Ask yourself, "Within the Gospel theme that people are loved and forgiven, how do I hope people respond after they hear my sermon?"* Perhaps you hope they'll respond by sharing God's love and forgiveness, for example, by offering more of their time, talent, and treasure; or they'll see how harmful gossip is and stop; or they will see a particular view and action on a social issue (choose your favorite) is in keeping with the Gospel.

2. *Imagine 100 percent of your listeners are persuaded by your message and responding as you had hoped.* Imagine when you see your listeners individually and in groups they tell you what persuaded them. You

might feel cordial, peaceful, and respectful toward them with a sense of camaraderie that you're "in" the Gospel together.

3. *Now imagine* no one *is persuaded by your message and they are not responding as you had hoped.* Imagine when you see your listeners individually and in groups they tell you why they are not persuaded.

4. *As you imagine them to be unpersuaded, how would that feel?* Maybe it would not matter to you. But if you think you would feel defensive, frustrated, scared, or angry; tempted to shame or offer a "this way or else" ultimatum; or if you would want to argue, undermine, or talk behind their backs, these feelings may indicate part of the sermon was used for a purpose other than to spread the Gospel. Because, even if you believe getting upset when people turn down the Gospel is justified, for *whom* is it justified? Ultimately, is it the preacher's job to persuade, or is it God's? Preachers plant seeds. We have no idea into what kind of soil the seeds will land, or what will happen to them in the next five minutes, five decades, or five eternities.

Whether imagined or real, defensive reactions suggest the sermon was not offered in perfect freedom. If we preach in perfect freedom, then we can *hope* for a particular response but let *God* be concerned about the *actual* response, even if it costs us dearly. If we preach a sermon of love and forgiveness in perfect freedom, then we will love our listeners just the same whether they are persuaded or not.

The message you have to offer from your *lectio*, prayer, study, and heart, is sufficient. Not only is what you have to offer sufficient, it's what your listeners really want to hear. You're the pastor they know. You're the priest they trust. You're the one they look to to learn how to live in God's good graces because of, and in spite of, who they are and the struggles they face. This is hard to believe for many preachers who struggle with the "who do I think I am" gremlin. Not trusting in their own voice, they quote others to shore up the validity of their sermons. But quoting others' words isn't necessary to offer a "real" message. It can be helpful, but it's not necessary. No matter how esteemed, respected, saintly, or erudite authors may be, their perspectives don't carry the weight of your words. It's not necessary to comb the internet for ideas, anecdotes, nor recite scholarly wisdom. When you trust that who you are and your spiritual and scholarly preparation is enough, then you know additional sources might serve as useful embellishment but won't make your message any truer.

This brings us to the juncture of authenticity and manipulating people's trust. In short, they don't mix. When we're comfortable with the prayerfulness and scholarship of our sermon preparation and the freedom inherent to its message, then we see the great dangers inherent to plagiarism, cherry-picking ideas, or fearing disagreement.

*Plagiarism.* Plagiarism is unethical because we don't give someone their due credit, but even more so because we manipulate people to believe something about us that isn't true. We're motivated by a belief that, by fooling our listeners, we will gain something—like a better reputation or job security. Plagiarism is unethical because it manipulates words to serve us rather than the Gospel. This is why I am utterly opposed to lifting a sermon off the internet when a "good enough" sermon is needed. Manipulating listeners' trust to save our reputation is never an option.

*Cherry-picking.* To trust in our authentic belief in the Gospel also means there's no need to cherry-pick to make a point. I hear cherry-picking usually happens in two ways. One is the choice of statistics and the other in the selection of Bible verses.

*Statistics* in sermons can be helpful. It's not that statistics should never be used, but it's as easy to be manipulated by them as it is to manipulate others. This is one reason stats can be problematic: "One view is no view." This is a reference to my husband's radiology world. It means one view of an organ seen in an X-ray is no view because it only presents one side. What's cancer free on one side of your kidney could be riddled with it when viewed from the other.

Statistics are tricky, especially if we read only one "view" from one source and if we only give one "view" in a sermon. Fifty percent of marriages in the United States end in divorce, right? Actually, go look it up.[4] It's not nearly as cut and dried as the number suggests. That's an easy example of a commonly quoted statistic, and we're remiss if

---

4. Abigail Abrams, "Divorce Rate in U.S. Drops to Nearly 40-Year Low," *TIME*, December 4, 2016, http://time.com/4575495/divorce-rate-nearly-40-year-low; Renee Stepler, "Led by Baby Boomers, Divorce Rates Climb for America's 50+ Population," Pew Research Center, March 9, 2017, http://www.pewresearch .org/fact-tank/2017/03/09/led-by-baby-boomers-divorce-rates-climb-for -americas-50-population; Bella DePaulo, "What Is the Divorce Rate, Really?" *Psychology Today*, February 2, 2017, https://www.psychologytoday.com/blog /living-single/201702/what-is-the-divorce-rate-really.

we don't verify its accuracy before repeating it. When we don't know there's more to the issue, we might accidentally offer only "one view."

We might offer one view by accident, but we might be tempted to offer only one view if that view supports a personal opinion. If you're thus tempted, ask yourself what's at stake if a more complex picture were offered. What if a second "view" rebutted the first one? What's your intention to use the statistic, and what's at stake to you, personally, if someone isn't persuaded by that statistic or your point of view?

Finally, there's another problem with the use of stats that has nothing to do with manipulation, but practical human nature. If we quote statistics, some of our listeners will stop listening because they'll argue with us in their heads. Some will pull out their phones to fact-check, and someone will be able to find a number to refute the evidence we present. Instead of helping to back up our point, statistics can become a distraction.

The easy question about using stats in sermons is to ask whether they are needed at all. Are they helpful or necessary? Does it matter if *50 percent* of all marriages end in divorce? Or is it enough to make the point that *many* marriages end in divorce? Is it the number that matters, or is there something even deeper, a universal human condition that's the real purpose of the message?

*Bible verses.* I could almost repeat the above paragraphs but substitute "Bible verse" for "statistic." To preach, obviously, Bible verses are necessary, but many verses contradict one another. They were written at different times of God's history with humanity. What people learned about God was layered one lesson on top of the other until, over the centuries, Scripture became like a Grand Canyon of sediment. The weight of some layers sifted into and mixed with others, while other layers remained intact, and all of them are beautiful. We can't always distinguish where one layer ends and another begins, but we can see the river of God's love and forgiveness cuts through them all.

What's a preacher to do when layers are indistinguishable, when verses contradict each other or our experience of God? Hike to the rim to view the whole canyon. The *whole* canyon reveals the beauty, love, forgiveness, complexity, sorrow, and joy of the intersection of God with humanity over eons, and no one layer reveals all. Because no one layer of rock reveals the whole canyon, and no one verse reveals the whole canon, to select one verse to be representative of God's intentions is risky at best and manipulative at worst. That's as misleading as pulling one rock from the bottom of the Grand Canyon to represent the sum effect of a vast, ancient story of water carving through rock. Often one verse is "one view," which doesn't represent the massive, ancient story of God's love and forgiveness carved through the human history.

If you're unsure, I encourage you to return to the questions above about how you'd feel toward your listeners if they disagreed with your interpretation, or offered different verses that suggested a different side of the story. What's at stake? When we preach authentically, we're not afraid to showcase what speaks against our point as much as what speaks in favor of it, nor are we afraid to offer a more complex or nuanced picture of the Gospel at work.

*Emotional manipulation.* In addition to plagiarism, statistics, and cherry-picking, when we preach authentically another tool we don't need is emotional manipulation. I remember the author Madeleine L'Engle wrote that while she was writing a book if something made her cry, she ripped up that section and started over. She never wanted to undermine the integrity of her craft or insult the dignity of her readers by inducing a predetermined reaction. Manipulating readers' emotions wouldn't serve to build their trust in her as their guide through the story.

If we're preaching with the intent to evoke a certain emotion or reaction, that's misleading and manipulative. Again, what's at stake for us to get that reaction? What does it mean if we do? What does it mean if we don't? We even have to be careful with humor. Funny sermons or anecdotes are useful as long as they illuminate the Gospel and aren't chosen to spotlight the preacher as comedian. If people are coming to hear you preach because they know they'll get a good laugh, then are they coming to hear you or hear Good News proclaimed?

Even so, to show I am a child of God who has not yet fully run the race set before me, here is the emotionally manipulative, preaching pipe dream I have nearly every time I preach at the early morning service. For no other reason than to discover whether it *can* be done, I'd like to find what it would take to move those early service attendees from expressionless stoicism to hearty belly laughs. Maybe the last sermon I preach when I retire could be granted license . . . ?

To recap, when we preach from the Word of God at the center of our inner labyrinths, we know what we have to offer is enough. Enough means we know what we offer doesn't need to be fancy, that we don't have anything to prove, and we don't need to make ourselves more or less than we are. As a result, to manipulate our listeners with plagiarism, cherry-picking, and emotional string-plucking is not only unnecessary, the choice doesn't cross our minds. We *know* the Word of God, filtered through us, is sufficient. Our sermon is sufficient and necessary, a gift we offer in perfect freedom.

### The Freedom of Limits

(Or, "I can do all things through Christ who strengthens me, except change the laws of physics.")

"I hate it that I need so much sleep," I whined to my therapist. "It wastes so much time! And unlike other people it seems, I can't function without it." I waited for her to commiserate. Sympathize. Or better yet, tell me the magic trick to managing without any sleep at all. No such luck. "Yes," she said simply. "You have limits."

*What was this psychological trickery?* I wondered. (OK, I cleaned that language up. I thought a different word than "trickery" at the time.) I was twenty-eight years old and in seminary. I wasn't old enough to have "limits!" I stared at her, stupefied, trying to comprehend some hidden allegory where "You have limits" really meant "You are limitless," while my stomach flipped into tangled Celtic knots of fear in case what she said might be true.

It was true, and it took me a while, several years in fact with setbacks to this day, to appreciate how liberating limits are. Limits are liberating because they let us state with integrity, "That's as much as I can do. I don't have to find an excuse because I've given all I've got. I can't add any more at the moment than I am able to add inches to my frame. Therefore, I stop."

*Clergy. Are not known. For embracing. Their limits.*

Until Jesus walks the planet again, there's no end to the work; there's always more ministry to do. Someone homebound to visit. Someone else who needs the Eucharist brought to them. Another email to be written and phone call made. Another volunteer to find, and you know you really should hang out with the youth group once in a while.

And then there are the expectations, spoken and unspoken, by your parishioners. How many of those expectations can you meet in a day, a week, a year, a decade? There's always something else, something different, something *more* you're supposed to be doing. Parishioners also tell you they want you to take care of yourself—you're working too hard, you're doing too much—until you *actually* take care of yourself and don't attend *their* meeting, *their* outreach, or *their* game night. *Oy!*

Then there are the expectations of yourself. The Second Coming hasn't happened yet and you see how much ministry is needed. You see your parishioners hurting; you genuinely care about them and wish you could be physically present instead of present only in spirit while you attend to more pressing needs.

You also want to preach well. To preach well requires time, quiet, study, prayer, creative writing time, practice, and revisions. Given the time needed to meet even some of the needs and expectations, where's the time for solid preaching going to come from? The math doesn't work. That's right. *The math doesn't work.* Therein lies the blessed restrictions.

If you're going to preach authentically then you only get to preach like a human being, who, like Jesus, slept, ate, hung out with his friends, escorted his mom to weddings, and went away for forty days to lose himself in God. And let's face facts: Jesus was only in ministry for three years and it killed him in the end. You're trying to do this ministry for a lifetime. If Jesus' time was so short to do his work and he accepted his limits, who do we think we are to ignore our own?

Before we go any further, I invite you to do an important exercise. I suggest you take as much time as you need to complete it, even if that means taking a couple of weeks, off and on, as you add thoughts to the worksheets. That's OK. It'll be worth it in the long run. Just don't let it slide because this can liberate you in astonishing ways to help you embrace your blessed limitations.

Directions: Complete Grids A–D in order. Answer the questions in each quardrant.

## *Where Does Preaching Fit?*

## Grid A

| **Formal Ministry Responsibilities**<br>(List what you were hired to do,<br>your formal job description.) | **Extra-Parish Responsibilities**<br>(List Board seats; denominational<br>duties; local outreach; ecumenical<br>efforts, etc.) |
|---|---|
| **Personal Life Responsibilities**<br>(e.g., religious community or family<br>duties; exercise; errands; chores) | **What I Need to Preach at My Best**<br>(e.g., number of hours needed<br>for sermon prep; prayer; creative<br>inspiration; location) |

## *Where Does Preaching Fit?*

## Grid B

| | |
|---|---|
| **Additional, Explicit/Formal Preaching and Ministry Expectations**<br>(What other duties are you given by your senior clergy and/or lay leaders?) | **Additional Unspoken, Implicit/Informal Preaching and Ministry Expectations**<br>(What's "understood" you will do by senior clergy and/or lay leaders?) |
| **Personal Preaching and Ministry Expectations**<br>(What do you expect of and from yourself?) | **Personal Life Expectations**<br>(What do those closest to you expect from you personally, and of your preaching and ministry?) |

## *Where Does Preaching Fit?*
## Grid C

**Supports My Preaching,
No Change Needed**
(From the "Grid A," three
"Responsibilities" sections, rewrite
the duties that support your best
preaching.)

**Supports My Preaching,
and Can Be Improved**
(From "Grid A," what duties
support your best preaching and
can be even better?)

**Hinders My Preaching
and Can Be Improved**
(From "Grid A," what interferes
with your best preaching that you
can change?)

**Hinders My Preaching
and Can't Be Changed**
(From "Grid A," preaching has to
work around these and there's no
getting around it.)

## *Where Does Preaching Fit?*

## Grid D

| | |
|---|---|
| **Supports My Preaching, No Change Needed** <br> (From "Grid B," rewrite the expectations that support your best preaching.) | **Supports My Preaching, and Can Be Improved** <br> (From "Grid B," what expectations support your best preaching but could be even better?) |
| **Hinders My Preaching and Can Be Improved** <br> (From "Grid B," what expectations interfere with your best preaching that you can change?) | **Hinders My Preaching and Can't Be Changed** <br> (From "Grid B," preaching has to work around these and there's no getting around it.) |

Now that you've completed this exercise, reflect on these questions:

What's working to support your preaching? What can you do to solidify that support to protect it? How many hours did you say you needed?

Look again at the formal and informal responsibilities and expectations. What's the *gap* between what you need to preach, the number of hours you require, and what can't be changed?

For example, let's say that your "best preaching self" needs about ten hours (as a working number. You may have determined you need a different number of hours for your best sermon prep. There's no correct number of hours other than the number you genuinely need.) of dedicated time each week to craft an effective sermon. However, between your official duties and unofficial expectations (of other staff, parishioners, and/or yourself), ten hours a week for sermon prep is "impossible." The gap can't be overcome. In that case, what happens typically is the ten hours either shrinks (increasing your stress); comes from the only other quadrant that's left, your personal life (also increasing your stress); or both (increasing your stress, and perhaps resentment, even more).

The laws of physics don't allow twenty-five pounds of potatoes to be stuffed into a five-pound bag. The math doesn't work. The laws of physics on this planet Earth dictate the math. For instance, the number of hours in a week is fixed. There are only 168, neither more nor less, and the truth is, Jesus won't return any sooner if you worked all 168. Moreover, there's the math for the amount of sleep you need and at which wee hours of night or morning. That's genetic. We can fudge it, but if we do we're not offering our best selves. There is also the math to indicate a rise in blood pressure due to stress because the sermon isn't done, like $170/95 > 110/60$. The higher number is not good. That math doesn't work well for your heart.

Now, back to the math for the ten hours you need for sermon prep. Go back through your quadrants. If you need ten hours, what can be tweaked? What can be given up altogether? If preaching is more important than other duties or expectations, what can you shift? What are the consequences if you do? If it isn't more important, own that. There are consequences to everything, good and bad, so what are they in this case? What can you live with? What can't you live with? What do you gain in terms of decreased stress and the level of your preaching if you *were* to find those ten hours? This exercise may require significant journaling, prayer, discernment, and discussions with your spiritual director. Take your time. Nothing will change in the meantime. Complete the exercise over time, finally filling in Grid "E."

## *Where Does Preaching Fit?*

### Grid E

| Based on the above, what will I change? | How will I do so and when? |
|---|---|
| | |

| Whom do I need to thank for supporting my preaching and preaching life? | Reflections |
|---|---|
| | |

Having completed Grid "E," did you find those "ten hours"? If so, you've made choices in favor of your preaching life. Great! Now you can skip the rest of this chapter. Blessed limits indeed!

If you're still reading, that means you didn't find those ten hours. Enter the blessed freedom of *your* limits . . . *and* your congregation's. Let me ask, Have you told your senior staff and lay leaders what it takes for you to prepare a sermon? Have you told them what you need to bring your best preaching self to the pulpit?

Most laypeople don't know what clergy do during the week. They certainly don't know what is required to craft a sermon. They don't know because many of us have never told them. Other clergy staff know what it takes for them to prepare an effective sermon, but they may not know what *you* need if you've never told them.

There are many reasons we don't raise our sermon needs with lay leaders or other clergy. One, it never occurred to us. (OK, that just changed.) Two, we don't want to sound like we're whining, complaining, or trying to get out of other work. (But unless you're a photon, you can't be in two places at the same time; and you're not a photon, so you can't. No matter how noble or blessed the intention, we can't work on a sermon single-mindedly while concurrently bringing the same holy attention to another ministry task. Those are blessed limits of brain and spiritual physiology. Therefore, we all have to make choices.) Three, we want to look like we work just as hard as everyone else. (Pride, vainglory, hubris, vanity, folly, and wind chasing. Did I miss any?) And four, even if we say what we need, we may wonder why we bother because we believe nothing is going to change. (That's the story you're telling yourself; is it a true story? And even if your assumption appears correct, doesn't Jesus change hearts and work miracles?)

Now we're getting to the crux of the matter, the gift of limits for the church. I suggest lay and clergy leaders conduct a similar exercise to the above grids. Rewrite the quadrants to name what lay and ordained leaders expect of their clergy, formally and informally, and what clergy expect of parishioners, formally and informally. That, in and of itself, would be revealing. You can open a big, beautiful, messy can of worms when you ask your lay leaders and senior staff to think about their own limits, the limits of the congregation and its finances, and the limits of the number of staff, the hours of work expected from each, and the priorities for the parish staff. Lay it all out in front of everyone and then together, make difficult, necessary, blessed, limiting choices.

As to the priority to be placed on preaching, according to a Pew research study reported in August 2016, "Fully 83% of Americans who have looked for a new place of worship say the quality of preaching played an important role in their choice of congregation."[5] This data suggests the *quality* of sermons matter when newcomers are deciding where they want to worship. If good preaching matters to the congregation (and it usually does), and if it matters to newcomers (as the Pew study suggests it does), then what time and resources need to be afforded to offer consistently effective preaching? What is given up to make this possible? What are the consequences of that? What compromises are required?

Limits are stressful to stick to in the moment, but they make life better in the long run. Brené Brown says, "Ninety seconds of discomfort is better than six months of resentment." Saying that uncomfortable "no" is far better than saying "yes" to long-term overwork, stress, and rising resentment.

To stick with popular figures for the moment, when you need to say "no," here's one of the most beautiful sentences of the English language I ever heard, and I learned it from Oprah Winfrey: "That doesn't work for me." Think about it! It's polite. It's respectful. It doesn't require an explanation. It leaves open the possibility that there's an alternative, and it suggests compromise and dialogue. That's the best no ever!

When faced with the choice of a new obligation or expectation, weigh it against what you need for your best preaching self to have the space and time to illuminate the Gospel in a troubled world. To which is God calling you? Ninety seconds of discomfort when you say, "That doesn't work for me," or another week spent in the Preacher's Panic Zone?

---

5. "Choosing a New Church or House of Worship," Pew Research Center, August 23, 2016, http://www.pewforum.org/2016/08/23/choosing-a-new-church-or-house-of-worship. And yes, this is a helpful statistic, and I suggest you read the whole article and not just take my word for it.

## Conclusion

Truly and nonjudgmentally, the place preaching has in your ministry is between you, God, and your congregation. We need to hear from you, from your backstory with God. We need to hear the sermon only you can offer that arises from the integration of your authentic self with the text. I hope it will be the best sermon it can be, one that will glorify God, rising from the depths of the Grand Canyon outward to the farthest star in the cosmos.

For it to be the best it can be, your prep requires your time, your single-minded and -hearted presence, prayer, and creative effort. There's a finite amount of those you can offer. Only you can figure out how much that is and make the most of them. That's another one of your limits. There's no guilt or shame in the result, only prayers for you to be as fully present to the Holy Spirit to guide you to speak the words your people most need to hear.

I believe that because there is only one of you, and because you were asked to preach, we need to hear *your* sermon. Please, don't deprive us.

# CHAPTER SIX

# Meditatio for Sermons

### Good News

The Good News is Scripture informs and forms us.

### Prayer

During sermon prep, I pray you consent
to be made into the Word of God you preach.

### Problem

*Umm* . . . sin.

### Vision

It is no longer you who preach, but Christ who preaches in you.

### Chapter in a Sentence

Become the Good News you preach.

### Latch

We go first.

(The workbook to integrate this chapter with your backstory and preaching
can be found at www.backstorypreaching.com.)

## Backstory

*"My soul magnifies the Lord,*
*and my spirit rejoices in God my Savior" (Luke 1:46-47).*

We go first.

*Lectio divina* beckons the preacher to go first to make the deep dive into Scripture. We go first to discover the uncomfortable truth of our human sinfulness and our vulnerability to be dependent upon God's love and grace. It's not pleasant, and it requires courage and a yearning for release from our sin by God to make the plunge. But we *also* go first to discover and accept God's mercy. That is very pleasant! We preachers go first to discover and experience the Good News ourselves. That's how we *know* the Good News is real. This is how we can stand with integrity to declare the Good News. Our integrity as preachers depends on our going first before we invite our listeners to go on the same journey. *Lectio divina* provides the map.

In the first stage of *lectio divina—lectio—*we give the text the chance to speak for itself. We let the people, puzzles, and possibilities percolate. We take note of our observations but give them time and space to breathe in our hearts, minds, and imaginations, holding our questions with reverence. But in *meditatio,* we *pursue* those questions, letting our curiosity get the better of us. We question with delight, relishing in and allowing the exploration and discoveries to change us into the Word we read.

Father Charles Curran, SJ, said that listening "involves a surrender of our world and a willingness to step into the world of another."[1] When we pray *meditatio,* we listen. We dive into our questions in order to listen to the world of others. We surrender ourselves to the wisdom and understanding others have offered as they also struggled to understand God in their worlds.

We first prepare ourselves to listen by giving up our egos, preconceptions, and wish lists for what we want the Scriptures to mean. We surrender ourselves when we listen to those who wrote about God in languages different from our own, or dive deep into a word study to capture nuances of thought. We ask questions and enter the social

---

1. Maria Tasto, *The Transforming Power of Lectio Divina: How to Pray with Scripture* (New London, CT: Twenty-Third Publications, 2013), 34.

and cultural contexts of Scripture and tradition to appreciate how God needed to act in their times and places, which might be very different from—or the same as—the way God needs to act with us. We also surrender ourselves when we listen to the explanations the text presents about itself when we follow footnotes, absorb commentaries, and check online resources.

*Meditatio* for sermon prep uses the same tools as the academic exegesis we learned in our training, but with a simple, profound difference. The intention of academic exegesis is to gather information so our sermons are grounded in the larger truth than the small truth of our personal thoughts and context. *Meditatio* for sermon prep does that and more. Because we listen and surrender ourselves to the worlds of others, we go first to fall into their stories of grace that are much larger than ourselves and our own time and place. We let ourselves be changed by others' worlds. In short, academic exegesis seeks to inform us; *meditatio* for sermon prep also seeks to form us.

Scripture was never intended to inform only, but to *form*. Scripture forms *a people*. Scripture forms us as a people by giving us an understanding of our common human nature, connecting us to that which is larger than ourselves, and most importantly, revealing and inviting us to take on our identity as God's beloved. Scripture creates our identity as children of God with a common history and shared purpose: to glorify the Author of Scripture and all Creation. *Meditatio* uses the critical tools of exegesis to gather information but with particular intentionality. We approach our inquiry with humility, vulnerability, and hope for "metanoia": to turn around, be enlightened, and thus formed into the Word of God we preach.

When we pray *meditatio*, we enter the text with a humble and open heart. We come with an attitude of trust and the scary-yet-exciting possibility to be molded more like Christ. We may feel the "thrill of the hunt" when we're searching for an answer, but in reality we're not *searching*; we're *beckoned*. We're beckoned by Love to draw us onward and closer, taking us to the people in Scripture who chased down our same questions and had the same yearning for God we have. We see their stories as our stories, their ordinary-extraordinary lives as our lives, and God's interest and interactions with them equally as transformative to our own.

We pray *meditatio* with a disposition like Mary's, "Let it be to me according to your word." In other words, "Yes, God. Whatever happens,

I'm in." When we say yes like Mary did and go "all in" to study and ruminate on the Word, the Spirit uses that time, the encounters with wisdom, and our yielding, to mold us. Indeed, were we to be handed a completed sermon that spared us our time and efforts it would do us—and our listeners—not only a disservice, but spiritual harm. Each time we engage in sermon prep, we start off on our own "Hero's Journey" (see chapter 8) and are changed in the process. We journey off into the text as one person, confront and repent of our sins, and emerge by grace as someone a little newer, someone a little more like Christ.

During *meditatio*, then, we ask questions that not only to deepen our knowledge but also to follow wherever it takes us into the depths of the human condition and the abundance of grace by contrast. In *meditatio*, the questions that yield the most fruit are "why" and "how." For example, why does this text matter? Why was it preserved, and why in this particular way, and for whom? How did these events come about? How was this possible? How could we have been so stupid, foolish, or arrogant? How could God have cared so much? Asking why and how after every answer helps us descend to ever deeper layers of meaning, understanding, and revelation.

We also ask what's at stake in the text. If the Good News asks us to give up an idol in exchange for God, then what's the idol in this text? What golden calf are we asked to throw on the fire? You'd think we'd rejoice to get one more calf dumped out of our closet to free up space, and yet often we hold back, thinking maybe, one day, we might still need it. Why? What's that about? Moreover, what's offered in exchange for the idol? What does God offer to trade for that golden calf? Love? Peace? Further divestiture of worldly goods that someone needs more? Might we receive compassion in exchange for dashing the bliss of our ignorance?

Preachers go first to listen to and surrender ourselves to the text. We let ourselves be beckoned forward into unknown territories of idols and grace, going further and further until we find ourselves at the crossroads of the human condition and God's mercy.

## Preaching

### *The Problem? The Human Condition of Sin*

We preachers need to be clear about our propensity to carry golden calves until it kills us. It reminds me of being a passenger in a cart pulled by sled dogs in Alaska on a summer training run. Even though the run was only two miles long I was surprised how often the musher stopped the dogs. She explained the dogs are so intent on running that during the warm summer months she has to stop them frequently to cool down or they would run to the point of heat exhaustion and death. Likewise, we are so intent on carrying as many golden calves as we can that we will carry them to the point of spiritual exhaustion and death. As preachers, we need to listen to the bitter and painful truth when we ask one simple question: Why? When Christ not only offers to take all those calves off our hands but did so already through his death and resurrection, why do we insist it's better to take them back?

Being able to articulate our messed-up rationale to carry idols juxtaposed against Christ's redemptive act is necessary because it underlies our understanding of the Gospel and humans' response to it. It's the lens through which we interpret the gap between humans as we are and the reign of God that is hoped for and promised. That, in turn, shapes the message of our sermons and the form each one takes.

This is my summary of the nature of human sinfulness. God perpetually invites us to believe and share the Good News, which is to forgive and love as we are forgiven and loved. Our problem is, we turn down God's invitation just about as often as it's offered.

We're invited by Jesus Christ to trust this Good News and build a reign of God based on compassion, mercy, and justice. However, we repeatedly decline the invitation, sometimes quite rudely and sometimes ever so politely. The character Elizabeth Swann in the comedic action movie *Pirates of the Caribbean: The Curse of the Black Pearl* offers one of the best-ever turndowns to an invitation. In response to the summons to have dinner with her pirate-kidnapper, she says, "I am disinclined to acquiesce to his request." Ah, yes, fools that we are, we are disinclined to acquiesce to God's requests to love and forgive as God does us. If you want a primer about the breadth and depth of the ways we turn God down, look to the Good Friday litany for a refresher on our creativity. Our imaginations seem to have no limit to our harebrained justifications to turn down God and the better, more peaceful, just, and loving existence God offers.

If the Good Friday litany can be likened to the "trees" of our sinfulness, the "forest" is the Great Commandment. Using the older language I grew up with that is seared on my heart, "You shall love the Lord your God with all your heart, with all your mind, and with all your strength. This is the first and great commandment, and the second is like unto it: You shall love thy neighbor as thyself." The Commandment begs the fundamental question: Can any one of us claim that at *all* times and in *all* places we love God and our neighbors like ourselves? (Indeed, as is often pointed out, do we even love ourselves to begin with?) The answer, of course, is a resounding "No," we don't love God or our neighbor like ourselves all the time and everywhere.

Prayer and spiritual disciplines increase our sensitivity that we do not love the way and extent to which God loves us, nor do we share that love as Christ shares it with us. As our sensitivity becomes more acute, we no longer need to judge the difference between "large" and "small" sins, or determine that one sin is "worse" than another. We ache with the self-inflicted wounds to our hearts whenever we turn God down or toss even the smallest stone for others to stumble over and question their faith. Size, degree, or comparison of sin cease to have meaning. There is only sin, and only God's mercy, and the bittersweet spiritual gift of compunction when our hearts are pierced simultaneously by the sorrow for our sin and the balm of grace.

The humility of deep, *gnosis*-kind of *knowing* that we don't live the Great Commandment is the great equalizer between human beings. When we venture into the text ahead of our parishioners to learn another ingenious way that we do not share God's love and are in need of still more grace, then we are *always* preaching to ourselves. It's never "us" and "them," but always and only "us." It's only Christ's mercy that unites us as one Body, humbled and forgiven. *Meditatio* beckons us to go first into the uncomfortable details of our sin and God's overwhelming mercy.

The preacher goes first in order to show our listeners that we are led by Christ to pass through the trials and tribulations of sin to the Promised Land. During *meditatio* we are shown God's grace, but also our sin, which lets us empathize with our listeners. We become the example of the "universal singular": what is true of my sin is true of all sin. We use ourselves as the example, but not by talking about ourselves in the sermon or baring our souls or skeletons, but with empathy and humility, as representative of the whole. We're no different from anyone else. There is no sin we have committed that others haven't. Acknowledging our sin to God during *meditatio* grants us empathy with our listeners.

The uncomfortable truth of the human condition is this: If the Good News is so good, why don't you and I and everyone else accept it? The very short answer is, because we don't accept we're loved with all the love God has to give. If we did accept all that love for us and for *all*, our closets would be emptied of their golden calves and we would serve Christ in each person selflessly, gladly, and respectfully. But our universal human condition doesn't fully accept God's love and that drives us to every flea market in a five-hundred-mile radius to add some new golden calves to our already bulging closets. We need a lot of persuading that a closet silent and emptied of calves is better than a full and cacophonous one. Sermons need to help us feel what it's like to be *inclined* to acquiesce to God's request to let Jesus lead those calves away.

To let Christ do his work, during *meditatio* we ask questions like the following.

1. What? *What is our problem?* Describe the stumbling block. What do we see in the biblical characters and, thus, in ourselves that is contrary to God's hopes for us? For example, God tells us to rest on the Sabbath, but what do we do instead? We work and do all kinds of things that don't contribute to honoring God or toward our rest and renewal. We do what we want rather than what—God knows!—we need. What motivates us to go our own way instead of accepting what God says is best for us? Paint the picture of our shiny golden calf.

2. Why? *Why do we love ourselves more than God?* Why do we pit ourselves against our neighbors and try to make God love us more than God loves them? Why do we do mental and spiritual gymnastics to make ourselves believe that loving ourselves over and against others is in our best interest? To pick up on the Sabbath example, why do we believe work is more important than rest? No one has more work to do than God, yet God rests! Why do we buy into the idea that our labors are more important or necessary than God's? Keep asking why until you can give the sin its name.

3. What's the vision? *What life does God imagine for us that's better than our life now?* The vision describes the reign of God. What would it feel like to live in the reign of God? What would "peace" and "love" and "justice" and "rest" look like in real life? Use all five senses to make the vision real. For instance, what would a Sabbath life look like, and how is the vision of Sabbath rest loving? What would our lives be like if we actually did the things we needed to

renew our spirits? How might we be different? How would we love others differently than we do now? Describe our new home in the Promised Land.

4. How? *How do we get there?* If people have been persuaded so far by the sermon, then they need to know how to get to the Promised Land. This is to describe the way, the truth, and the life of Christ. Christ bridges the gap from where we are now to the place God hopes and plans for us to be.

"How do we get there?" can be viewed as choices among metaphorical maps. The map selected is based on the particular leg of the journey to the Promised Land described in the sermon. For example, one map might show only the first few steps as we start out, hopeful, relieved, excited, but scared too. Or the map might show the middle of the journey, when the novelty has long since worn off and we're tired, dirty, crabby, and clinging to a diminishing hope. Or perhaps we're closer to the end. Do we see the Promised Land over the next ridge? We're so close! Or have we arrived and need to build a new home and put down roots?

"How do we get there?" is not vague as if gesturing with our arm that we're headed "somewhere over there." For instance, let's say the sermon persuaded us to yearn for weekly Sabbath rest. We can see its possibilities over the next ridge. We feel the hope, indeed the reality, of Sabbath. A detailed, close-up map might include suggestions to divest ourselves of some of the things we believe we "have" to do and reconsider true-life possibilities of what genuine rest might include. On the other hand, a bigger, more general map might consider our spirits, motives, and established patterns. A general map might point out our hubris that more work makes us feel more godlike, and lead us to ask for the humility to be human, accept our limitations, and put our feet up. Another general map might ask why patterns are the way they are; for instance, why are lay leaders' meetings scheduled after church, or why are kids' soccer tournaments scheduled for Sunday mornings? It's not enough to trust that there is a Promised Land out there somewhere. Listeners also need a sense for how we can get from Point A to Point B with Jesus at the head of the wagon train.

This is why I am rarely persuaded by sermons that end with "Let us _____" or "May we _____" (as in, "Let us go now to honor the Sabbath" or "May we always honor the Sabbath."). Sermons that end with "Let us" feel like the preacher forgot to pick up the map on the way to church so has to end with an implicit "Good luck with that." Listeners don't feel or see the vision of God's reign as a true, flesh-and-blood possibility, here and now. The "may-wes" make God's reign feel like a great idea but impossible to implement. This is one reason sermons are often perceived as irrelevant because they don't connect the message to the complexity of daily life. The may-wes don't direct us to pick up the bricks and mortar that will build an actual, new, holy reality, or conversely, the bricks and mortar to *be* the new, holy reality.

Let me expand on the point above to be sure I'm clear. I'm not suggesting sermons necessarily offer to-do lists to build the reign of God. This isn't a prescription for works-righteousness, guilt, or shaming. What I am suggesting is to take seriously what happens when a person encounters Jesus Christ in a sermon.

In the Bible, every person who encountered Jesus had to respond. Jesus called something out of every person and they had to deal with him. They had to make something of this man and his teachings and miracles. Jesus didn't fit established patterns. People had to wrestle with his disconcerting presence, words, and actions. People had to decide whether to listen to Jesus more, ponder his words, pretend the encounter never happened, chalk him up as a quack, throw rotten tomatoes at him, or follow him to his cross and empty tomb. They had to decide what to do with this odd man who, against all odds, claimed to be the Son of God and beat the certain odds of death.

Sermons throw us into an encounter with Jesus Christ and we have to decide what to do with him. Through the Word offered in the sermon, Jesus shows us there is Good News right now and immediately asks us to follow his way of love, compassion, and forgiveness. Jesus also shows us there is even better news: the Way to the Promised Land, a way to live and be that's better than the way things are now. In every sermon, we bring Jesus and listeners together into the same room so Jesus can disrupt established patterns in order to make better ones. Listeners have to decide what to make of the disruption and the new patterns Jesus lays down. After the preacher puts Jesus and our listeners face-to-face for most of the sermon, the conclusion says, "Now what?"

Meeting Jesus means something more disruptive than, "May we all remember and honor the Sabbath." Sermons hold in one hand the way things are now, like the reality of Sundays: soccer tournaments scheduled at the same time as worship, the need to work a second job on Sundays in order to feed the kids, and catching up with friends over brunch because that's the only time schedules mesh. So we show how things are now in one hand, while in the other hand, we hold up the Gospel and say, "Yes, Sundays are busy. *And* the Sabbath is a commandment to honor God and live one day differently from the other six. What do you make of that?" We and our listeners squirm a bit to see exposed the patterns we live compared to the patterns prescribed in the Gospel. The end of the sermon is more powerful when we describe new patterns, a new vision about priorities, use of time, or how Sabbath rest is different from the absence of work.

This is when we have the chance to move from "church talk" to being real. Preachers often gloss over the "What do you make of this encounter with Christ?" because we, too, are asked to consider new patterns and don't know how to stitch them into real life either. For example, not only did God command us to rest, but Jesus tell us that "Sabbath is made for humankind, not humankind for the Sabbath" (Mark 2:27-28). Jesus disrupted an established pattern about the Sabbath and now you, like everyone else, has to respond. You have to ask yourself questions like, If the Sabbath is made for humankind, what does that imply for Sabbath rest and keeping the day holy and set apart? Where in your life do you crave Sabbath? What does "rest" look like? What would it take for you to create Sabbath? What established patterns hold you back? What idols prompt you to work without ceasing? What does God have to say to you about that idol?

To wrestle with such uncomfortable disruptions starts with us, because if we're not willing to wrestle with them why should our listeners? Moreover, we have to wrestle with these questions so when it's time to select an illustration, we can tell whether the anecdote or story rings true. Indeed, if we don't wrestle with these new patterns Christ presents, then it's easy to fall back on vague theological platitudes that give the impression that the Promised Land is so theoretical as to be the Impossible Land.

We need the incarnational reality of the living Christ. Christ was made flesh; we are Christ's body in the world now, so there has to be a flesh and blood response available. This is what makes a sermon relevant and keeps listeners' attention. When we show the living Christ disrupts our patterns of sin and replaces it with patterns of holiness not as an abstract theory, but in flesh and blood, acting and being in us. Even and especially when a sermon invites our change of heart, a metanoia, that's what begins to change the world in our time and place—because we now see Christ in it, we are Christ in it. That can be plenty for one sermon.

Discerning all this for a sermon is very hard work. Let me say that again. This is very hard work! It's hard to discern the reign of God, it's hard to figure out why we turn down God's invitation, and it's hard to figure out how to respond to that invitation with a wholehearted "Yes" and actually be transformed into a living word of Christ. Because it's hard, preachers go first.

## Conclusion

*Meditatio* guides us to look for patterns of meaning. Patterns about the way things are now, and the new patterns that Jesus offers. We look for the patterns of resistance to change, and the patterns of holiness that result when patterns are transformed. The information we gather when we study Scripture is allowed, by grace, to form the preacher first into someone new, someone who looks and speaks more like Christ. By going first, we carry the map, walk alongside, and tell the other travelers that we've seen the Promised Land. Preacher and listener integrate Good News into our whole lives and preach it together.

### Guide to *Meditatio* for Sermon Prep

1. Prepare yourself with your sermon prep ritual.
   Pray to listen and surround to the Word so that it will no longer be you who preach, but Christ who preaches in you. Pray for courage, wisdom, and humility to follow wherever you are led, and for gratitude when you meet Christ.

2. Read the text again and refer to your *lectio* notes.
   Based on your *lectio*, what questions did you have? What piqued your curiosity most? What tugged at your heart? What irks you about the text? What hope is offered that you want God to realize?

3. Let yourself be led.
   - Here are suggestions of paths to find answers, but not necessarily in this order and not necessarily all of them for every sermon. Trust your gut, your instincts, and your interest.

- Read what is before and after the text in Scripture.
- Follow the footnotes.
- Do word studies, read the text in different languages, and read different versions of the Bible.
- Read about a character from start to finish.
- Learn the historical context, the author, and for whom the book was written.
- Look at the geography, the social context, and the actual scene. Be a "movie director" and "film" the action so you can "see" how they're dressed, who moves where, who speaks to whom, in what tone of voice, and in what order.
- Use your five senses and your pastoral intuition. Name what you can see, touch, hear, feel, and smell. Put yourself in the scene. What does your sixth sense tell you what's going on?
- What motivates people to do what they do? Use your imagination. What would motivate you if you were in the situation?
- What's *not* written about? What is left unsaid? Similarly, what is written in response to a conversation we missed, as Paul's letters do, for example. What did we miss?

4. Identify the human condition (the problem).
   - What's our problem? What's the universal sin revealed? What's the idol we don't want to give up? Why do we cling to it?
   - Keep asking "why," drilling deeper and deeper to find the core. Keep going until you find the moment of compunction, when you feel and know yourself to be both sinner and someone who is forgiven.
   - Name the problem.

5. Identify the Good News.
   - What does God offer? What is the Good News?
   - What is promised? What's the vision of the reign of God? Be concrete. Use your five senses, your heart, and your intuition to make it real and incarnational. The reign of God might ask us to take concrete actions, or change our hearts, or change our perspectives to see the world differently, but all make the Love of God real and shareable.

- What would make the invitation irresistible? Why would you say yes?
- Write the Good News in one sentence.

6. Rest in *contemplatio*.

   - Listen to the recording you made of your text again today. A good time is before you go to sleep, so the text is ruminating in you while you rest.
   - Have a way to record your thoughts upon waking.

(For more practical suggestions, the workbook to integrate this chapter with your backstory and preaching can be found at www.backstorypreaching.com.)

# CHAPTER SEVEN

# Preach, Come What May

### Good News
The Good News is when Christ dwells in us and we in him,
we care more about proclaiming the Gospel than we do about ourselves.

### Prayer
I pray you see that when it is no longer we who preach but Christ who preaches in us,
we're prepared to preach the Gospel no matter what.

### Problem
Self-preservation

### Vision
We are so filled with Christ's empathy and compassion we overflow with courage.

### Chapter in a Sentence
When we focus on Christ, we can't not preach.

### Latch
A story

(The workbook to integrate this chapter with your backstory and preaching can be found at www.backstorypreaching.com.)

## Backstory

*"When the Advocate comes, whom I will send to you from the Father . . . You also are to testify because you have been with me from the beginning" (John 15:26-27).*

She *quivered* with rage. I had never seen anyone *quiver* with rage, let alone in response to one of my sermons. But she quivered all right, as much as any aspen tree.

The first out the door after the early morning service, she walked between me and the adult servers. She stopped for only a moment. Shorter than I, she turned up her face, eyes radiating outrage, to spit, "I do *not* want *those* people in my church!"

Another first for me. I had heard of people uttering that sentence, but in twenty-five years of ordained ministry I had never heard it myself. And the funny thing was, I didn't preach about including *those* people in our church.

But what I did or didn't preach didn't matter to my body. My face instantly flushed red in shame with the accusation, my vision narrowed, and I left my body ever so slightly. I felt attacked, shocked, scared, and self-protective, and my mind flashed across my sermon in a nanosecond wondering, "*Had* I said that?" I knew I hadn't and all I could think of was to bluster defensively, "I didn't say that!" which was immediately echoed in agreement by the servers. The parishioner shot back, "Oh, yes you did, yes you did!" and she tornadoed out the doors.

The funnier thing that's not funny at all was that if I had preached what she thought I had preached, I would be willing to proclaim that message with a bullhorn: "*Those* people *are* welcome in this church!" So why did I feel ashamed? Why did I second-guess myself the rest of the morning? Why did I check with several people to ask what they had heard and was the sermon OK? Why, I hate to admit, do I still consider her every time I write a sermon and wonder whether I'll be verbally attacked again?

On a different Sunday years ago, I preached against the death penalty in my congregation in Indiana, a death penalty state. Separately, three men approached me about the sermon, incensed that I had mixed politics and the pulpit. All were taller and bigger than I. One, in fact, was a former NFL linebacker who sported a Super Bowl ring. As each bent over me, they didn't quiver in rage but I quivered a little in fear (especially under the linebacker). Even though I knew they wouldn't physically harm me, my body was trying to *get me out of there!*

I could go on, but I'm sure you get the picture. The truth of being a preacher is, we are called to preach the Gospel no matter what and that means people are going to react when the Gospel rubs them the wrong way. People's reactions can be a one-off or a sustained campaign. Their reactions can be scary, hurtful, manipulative, passive-aggressive, directed at us, above us to our superiors, toward or around us on social media, or all of the above.

So, remind me. *Why* do we do this?

Why do we do this to ourselves? Why do we put ourselves out there, a target for public reaction? Why do we make ourselves the Rorschach tests of people's projections, perceptions, and interpretations? Why do we put ourselves in the position in which we might receive nonsensical or self-righteous outrage? Why do we offer sermons that stir the waters instead of stroking them to keep them calm?

The short answer is, we do it because Jesus did it. Jesus preached the Gospel no matter what. He preached Good News whether the message was welcome or not, and that means we have to too. (Do I hear an "Amen," or do I hear an "Oh, *rats*" . . . or is that just me?)

Knowing the potential consequences, how do we find the courage?

There's a story about St. Francis. He asks his Brother Leo to write down what he is about to tell him about the nature of true joy. Francis dictates that true joy is not to swell the ranks of the order with bishops, theologians, or kings, or to convert unbelievers. Nor, he continues, is true joy the gift to heal the sick or perform miracles. Surprised, Brother Leo asks him what true joy is, then. Francis responds by describing the following scene.

Francis returns to the friary on a cold, wintry night, cold enough that icicles have grown on the bottom of his muddy habit and cut his legs until they bleed. He approaches the gate and knocks for a long time. One of his brothers finally comes to the door and demands that the knocker identify himself. Francis says that it is he, Francis, and begs entrance for the love of Christ. Yet without explanation, his brother repeatedly refuses Francis admission. As Francis remains waiting at the door, the brother hurls abuses at Francis. When Francis stays, the brother clubs him! Without response or defense, Francis continues to wait at the door for entry.

Francis concludes to Brother Leo, "I tell you that if I kept patience and was not upset—that is true joy and true virtue and the salvation of the soul."[1]

At first glance, this may seem an antiquated notion of faithfulness akin to hair shirts, or a modern notion of codependence or stupidity. Or, Francis's reaction may smack of a saintliness that none can achieve except for extraordinary souls like he, a saint elevated to such a level that he didn't mind the dark, the hunger, the cold and mud, nor his bleeding legs.

This is not what we see when we look deeper. David Rensberger, in his article "True and Perfect Joy," points out several important aspects of this story. Rensberger notes that the one who denies Francis entry is a brother. They are connected through their vows to be members of the same household, and Francis does not disavow the connection. Another noteworthy observation is, Francis does not try to persuade his brother to let him in, nor does Francis defend himself or try to prove he is falsely accused. Ultimately, Rensberger writes, "I don't see this story as being about remaining in an abusive relationship as if that were somehow 'the Lord's will.' Rather, it teaches that *spiritual joy does not come from happiness and achievement and success*—'even the Gentiles' (Matt 5:47) could manage that, after all—*but instead arises from remaining intent on Christ* through pain and difficulty and betrayal. Francis aspired to yield, like Jesus, to the will of God that he perceived to be somehow present underneath this undeserved affliction."[2]

Francis was not intent on changing his brother to become a "better" brother. Nor was he focused on forcing his way in to get near the fire just inside the locked doors, or to the hot food kept warm on the kitchen stove. Nor was Francis concerned to save his reputation, prove himself right or his brother wrong. Instead, Francis waited at

---

1. From Archivum Franciscanum Historicum, Chapter 8, "Little Flowers of St. Francis," quoted in "The Joy of Peace," December 2000, *Crib and Cross Franciscan Ministries*, http://cribandcross.org/the-crib-and-cross-archive/the-joy-of-peace-december-2000.

2. David Rensberger, "True and Perfect Joy," *Weavings*: *A Journal of the Christian Spiritual Life* 27, no. 4 (2012): 20. Emphasis mine.

the door; he waited on Christ, and on Christ alone. By focusing on Christ, Francis' vision was filled with Jesus' perfect love. This perfect love cast out Francis's fear about what would happen next. In light of Jesus' perfect love, what happened next wasn't important; there was only now, Christ, and a brother who suffered too.

In spite of and because of his suffering, Francis kept focused on the Christ who had suffered dearly. While Francis suffered he kept vigil with Christ while Christ was rejected, falsely accused, and beaten. Francis's gaze was fixed on Christ, whose perfect love gave Jesus compassion for those who caused the suffering as much as for those who suffered. As a result, Francis could see the suffering his brother doorkeeper endured. The doorkeep's hardness of heart was a terrible burden that compromised his humanity. Francis, like Jesus, had compassion for his brother, and Francis, like Jesus, forgave him.

Focused and filled with Christ, Francis did not fear for himself— all was right in his spirit. But Francis did fear for the welfare of his brother in whom all was *not* right in his spirit. Francis was not afraid; miserably uncomfortable, yes, but not afraid. With his focus on Christ and his brother's well-being, Francis had no mental bandwidth left to concern himself with himself. Francis accepted the suffering and did not fear what was to come, because to focus on Christ and his perfect love for his brother was the only thing there was *to* be done.

Return now, to my quaking, outraged parishioner. See her through Christ. Jesus loves her. He does not fear her. He is her kin, and she, his. Through baptism in Christ, she is my kin, and I, hers; we are sisters in Christ.

She is also attached to "her" church, to our congregation; they matter profoundly to her. Something I preached frightened her. Something I preached felt like a threat to "her" church. The idea that *those* people could enter her sanctuary violated something important to her, something she holds dear. She feared she might lose something—in her eyes, something was at risk.

"Her" church was at risk. In order for the church to be "hers," she had to have created a definition of what that meant. She had to have set a standard, an ideal, that made it "her church." Based on the strength of her reaction, her fear wasn't only that *those* people would lower the standard, but that the standard would be shattered into something unrecognizable, perhaps beyond repair. The church would no longer be "hers," and she would lose something sacred and worth protecting.

"Her" church is sacred enough that the threat she perceived sent her limbic system into overdrive. From the moment her "flight, fright, or freeze" hormones went into hyperdrive, she was literally unable to hear what I said. She was so frightened, she could trust only the fears her mind kept looping. She could not interpret the sound waves made by my vocal cords when they vibrated her eardrums; she could not hear what was actually said in the sermon. Nor could she accept the evidence offered to the contrary in my stuttered denial and the denial's reinforcement by two witnesses. She was still so enthralled by fear she could only *feel* "Danger, danger!"

In my mind's eye I see her fear. I see her trapped by her assumptions, unable to see the image of God's face in the faces she fears, faces that are different from her own, faces of people whose manner of dress and life experience is anathema to her. I want her to find joy in the images of God they carry, to learn she need not worry about protecting God or the church from *those* people. She need not protect herself from them. She is safe. God is equally well pleased with her whether *they* are there or not.

Now, in your mind's eye, see me through Christ. Jesus loves me. Jesus is kin to me, and I to him. Through baptism in Christ, I am kin to the parishioner as my sister. I, too, was frightened. My body reacted like my sister's did. My limbic system was concerned about my survival. Even though there was no actual danger to my life or limbs, my limbic system didn't care. Survival hormones are nonpartisan, nonsectarian, unbiased, and scrupulously equal. They treat every perceived threat the same. I couldn't manage the way my body reacted to her rage any more than my sister could manage her perceived threat. I was so shaken I could not trust the truth about what I knew I said or didn't say, which caused me to seek reassurance throughout the morning. My sister and I both had our survival instincts hyperreact to an imagined threat neither of us could control.

Moreover, and I don't like to admit this to myself or to you, but she threatened *my* church. I, too, had something at risk. "My" church *includes those* people, and it does *not* include *those* people who deny *those* people an equal place at the table. Were *my* church filled with *those* people who deny *those* people, I, too, would feel I were losing something precious, something sacred. I would lose my sense of place, of belonging. Indeed, my unwelcome relocation from my hometown in the Upper Midwest to the Bible Belt for my husband's job was a shock to my system for these very reasons. Truthfully, the first time my family and I attended the local Episcopal church whose piety and theology were so different from my own, I wept while crying out to God, "You mean, I have to give up my church too?" I was inconsolable for weeks.

Like my sister, I am bound by my fears. Like her, I perceive threats, not only to *my* church, but also to my integrity. I wanted to prove she was wrong, that she had accused me falsely. That I would be willing to say what she *thought* I said in another sermon didn't matter; I still wanted to prove her wrong, such is my ego.

So here we are, my sister and I. Both bound by our fears, both care about our "churches," she for "her" church, and me for "my" church. We both want to succeed as the Gentiles do to convert and add one another to the ranks of the other's "church." She suffers in her fear and wants to change me. I suffer in my fear and want to change her. We both want to protect and guard our respective "churches." So we suffer together in our fears, my sister and I. We are not so different after all.

Preaching stirs up our fears. Sometimes those fears are more tingly and exciting than scary, like the thrill to learn we're actually, deeply, truly loved. But sometimes preaching is more like stirring a nest of fire ants. Many of us only have to offer a social justice sermon for those fears to come pouring out every which direction, ready to defend their innate need to survive.

Sermons mess with our fears because Christ offers to take away idols we hold dear. The more dearly held the idol, the more Christ's offer to free us from them feels less like Good News and more like a threat. Every sermon asks us to walk to Golgotha to toss our golden calves into a junk pile at the foot of the cross, and as a species, we're not easily persuaded. We don't want to give up our golden calves called "my church," or our justifications for our entitlements, self-preservation, or self-selected tribe. Rather than give up those idols at the cross, we talk to Jesus as he hangs there, trying to persuade him that what he was really teaching us was how to fill our arms with golden calves and carry his cross at the same time.

But our fear to give up our idols in itself binds together preacher and listener. We suffer together for the sake of setting down our idols in exchange for a bigger piece of the cross. It's unavoidable, and even though we know this, we wish the suffering away as if breaking free the Gospel didn't involve the painful destruction of our idols. We fear the suffering that comes with carrying the cross. We also fear to accept that suffering for Christ's sake is as normal and anticipated as Lent giving way to Easter.

When we preach about the one true God, by implicit comparison our sermons reveal the untruth of false gods. The fictitiousness of idols reveals itself when contrasted with the truth of the living God, because to preach truth is de facto to identify lies. In the very act of carrying the cross, the comparison with not carrying idols is made and the threat implied. When in the thrall of idols, any of us can and do act as the idols' minions to do "battle" with those who bear the cross.

We do need great courage, then, to preach a Gospel that will place us between our listeners and their beloved idols. We need courage—meaning, to feel afraid and preach anyway. Yes, we need courage on the one hand because at times we will be afraid *and* we need to preach anyway. We need courage because we'll be afraid, knowing a sermon will stir up a tempest in a particular listener or maybe in all our listeners. We need courage when we know the Good News won't feel good for some but more like that proverbial last straw, causing some never to pledge again or darken our church doors. We also need courage because we will be afraid for ourselves when former linebackers unexpectedly lean over us, yell, and punch the air with their index fingers next to our faces. We need courage to preach because our limbic systems will protect us just like they're supposed to and on cue. True enough, we need courage at both times: when we knowingly walk into a tempest, and when we get surprised because we didn't notice the first stirrings of air that promised the storm.

So yes, on the one hand, yes, we need courage. On the other hand, we need courage, *but* . . .

*But* we don't really need courage because here's the simple truth about preaching: When we are overcome by the Gospel, we speak Jesus' words because they must be said. When we dwell in him, and he in us, we love more perfectly. When we love more perfectly, we do not fear for ourselves or the consequences. Along with Jesus, we may be hauled to the edge of the cliff by the mob and threatened to be tossed over. We fear for our lives. Yet we're OK with whatever happens next because there's something else we fear even more: to leave Christ's words unsaid. Those words are too valuable, too saving, too liberating, too loving. They *must* be said. Out loud. Whether people listen or not, react or not, are indifferent or converted, fall prostrate on the floor, drop a check for $100K in the offering plate, or are driven wild with fury and carry us to the edge of that cliff, Jesus' words spoken out loud into the atmosphere of this world matter more. They matter more than the outcome, whether those in thrall of their panic to protect their idols drop the preacher over a thousand feet of gravity, or let the preacher walk back through the midst of them.

When we absorb Jesus as the Word and let his words take over our speech until they are our own, we can't not say them. Our words become his words, and his are ours. Moreover, his love for his people becomes our love for his people. His compassion for them is our compassion. His forgiveness, mercy, and connection become ours, enough so that we don't care whether the rain falls equally on the righteous and the unrighteous, whether our sermons are heard accurately or inaccurately, or whether by those kindly toward us or by those unkindly. The need to protect our reputations is overwhelmed by the need to proclaim the Gospel, and we cease to consider whether accusations against us are false or accurate, or whether our sermon is preached in "my" church or "her" church. The Word *makes us* Good News, and we preach it.

Perfect love doesn't cast out the fear generated by our limbic systems. But perfect love does cast out the fear of anything that might dissuade us from preaching anyway. In other words, perfect love helps us decide what to do next by not focusing on real or imagined consequences, but by staying focused on living, being, breathing, and proclaiming Christ. That's why St. Francis's peace and joy were found waiting outside the monastery door. He wasn't waiting on his brother doorkeeper to change; he was attending to Christ. That's why Francis didn't fear what would happen next because as he was already in Christ, he had nothing to fear. To love perfectly and without fear means we announce Jesus Christ and his Good News in our sermons as the only thing we can do come what may, even when it makes us miserably uncomfortable.

My outraged parishioner will probably get mad again. I'm bound to stir her fears again, and she is bound to stir mine. We're in this together, after all, sisters that we are. So I will pray to be overcome by the Good News and filled with Jesus' perfect love, aware of the cost to speak his words, but swayed by the higher cost not to. Words of love and connection, liberation and mercy, joy, forgiveness, and peace uttered to include *those* people, *and* those people who don't want *those* people, Gospel words that will rain down equally on our unrighteous ears, mine and hers.

Come what may.

## Preaching

*"[W]oe to me if I do not proclaim the gospel" (1 Cor 9:16).*

To integrate our backstories of spirituality and life with the craft of preaching come what may, we need to humbly monitor our fiduciary duty as preachers, and empathize with our parishioners.

### The Preacher's Fiduciary Duty

Difficult sermons are difficult because they raise difficult emotions. When emotions rise, discretion lowers. When we feel passionately and believe we are in the right, it can be all too easy to walk up not just into the pulpit, but into the *bully* pulpit. The hard thing about anxiety-inducing sermons (in us and/or our listeners) is discerning whether the sermon is truly in service of the Gospel and our listeners, or whether we might be taking advantage to set them straight as measured against our personal plumb lines.

Many, if not all of us, have heard sermons in which the preacher castigated lay leaders for their attacks on that preacher, or lambasted the congregation for not pledging enough, or insisted that they must do "X" or else they're not "Christian." When a situation is emotionally raw, we can lose the judgment to discern whether we're pointing toward God's reign or toward our own.

The pulpit is a position of authority from God who offers Good News for *all* people, not those we select. Our job is to proclaim that Good News in a way that does not make us the center of attention, neither hero nor victim, as is often said. Nor are we allowed to channel our inner "Jeremiah" to abuse the authority vested in us and the people we serve. If we think our circumstance or prophetic voice is the exception to that rule, that's enough to tell us it isn't and we aren't. Before we bring our personal example into the pulpit or feel justified to be the "prophetic" voice against people also in need of God's grace, it's wise to vet the idea and the manuscript with two other preachers whom we know won't automatically agree with us.

To reiterate, I do not suggest we don't need prophetic or strong voices. As I write this in 2018, I believe our world is in desperate need of strong, prophetic voices, more so than most of us have seen in our lifetimes. *My point is, our fiduciary duty to place the needs of our listeners ahead of ourselves always trumps personal satisfaction.* Our personal convictions must be used *in service of* the Gospel and our people, and not for personal gain to vent our spleens. Because it can be so hard to tell where the personal stops and the corporate begins, the most responsible thing we can do is vet the ideas, theology, message, and implications in a sermon with people who will tell us the truth, and then have the humility to take what they say to heart and change course if needed.

One idea to get our raw feelings out of our system so we can be more present to the Spirit is to do what Brené Brown suggests in her book *Rising Strong* to write a "shitty first draft," or SFD for short. [3] (And if you find the "s-word" offensive, change it to "smarmy first draft.") Write down your unfiltered, raw feelings where no one will ever see them. We can take it another step as preachers to write the sermon we *wish* we could preach. *This* is the place to channel your inner Jeremiah, or your inner Mary (Virgin, Magdalene, or Bethany, as needed), or your inner finger-shaking, run-on-sentencing Paul! Keep a journal, or take your laptop to a park, or use newsprint and thick, colored markers. Bring tissues to mop the tears, and a glass of water to soothe the burning throat, and let it rip. Out loud. Written out. Draw pictures with bold strokes. No "shoulds, oughts, or holy thoughts" allowed. Blow your congested feelings out of your system so you can be openhearted again, not only to Christ's compassion for you, but to *all* whom you serve.

3. Brené Brown, *Rising Strong: The Reckoning, the Rumble, the Revolution* (New York: Spiegel and Grau, 2015).

A tip. A really important one. *Before you start, plan your exit strategy. Know where those pages or pixels are going to end up.* Plan to delete, burn, or put them in your safe-deposit box—just be certain you won't share them by accident.

After all this, if you still feel stuck emotionally and worry you might yet spew or gush, then get legalistic on yourself. Write this at the top of every sermon prep page: "I vowed in my ordination to uphold my fiduciary duty to serve others before myself. I will keep my vow and not force my personal views on them." Then ask a preaching buddy to read your final draft if you're not sure that you kept a lid on what needs a seal.

## *Empathy*

I'm going to borrow Dr. Seuss's "Star-Bellied Sneetches" for this illustration. For those unfamiliar, some Sneetches had stars on their bellies and some didn't. Those with stars were considered superior to those without them. An entrepreneur came to town with the ability to add or remove the stars. The result was mayhem as each group ran through his machine adding or removing their stars in a quest to become or remain "special."

Let's say you serve a congregation filled with snobbish Sneetches with stars on their bellies, all of whom believe in their fundamental superiority. You offer a riveting, persuasive sermon of equality, respect, and dignity for all Sneetches with and without stars. One family you know slightly heard the sermon and leaves outraged . . . except for the dad. The dad is persuaded. So much so that the next day he has his star removed in an act of solidarity with Sneetches who have none.

The dad lives in a family, comes from a family, lives in a neighborhood, works at a company, and worships at a church where nearly everyone has a star on their belly and believes in their superiority. When the dad shows up after deliberately having his star removed, at his home, at his parents', in his front yard, at work, and at church, how do you imagine he'll be received? However Sneetches welcome one another, it's a safe bet he won't be getting one.

When we preach the Gospel and hope (or even expect) people to "fall in line" with the obviousness of the Gospel's rightness, we can't know what following the Gospel will cost any one person. We can't know what it might cost their relationships with their families, at work, or in their neighborhoods. We can't know what it might cost their kids at school, the effect on decades-long friendships with people at church, or that they may feel they are betraying the traditions of their ancestry.

Think what would happen, for instance, were you to "change sides" politically, or on a social issue, or to a different denomination or religion altogether. What effect would that have on your relationships? The truth is, most of us at times keep our beliefs under wraps because we want to avoid rocking relationships we hold dear. Yes, some of us speak up "no matter what," but I'd guess even the most outspoken among us would hesitate if they felt they might burn *all* the bridges they've built with their family and community.

Most of us have our limits. For example, I had a spiritual directee who was more passionate in her love and dedication to God than nearly anyone I've known. Yet she was outspoken in her frequent repetitions to say that she would do anything God asked of her except love God more than she loved her children. This directee was unusual (in my experience) of those willing to articulate the limits to which they will follow Christ. Most of us won't admit them. Most of us have a line in the sand that we're willing to walk right up to, but not cross. We're willing to follow Jesus and risk "this" much on our side of the line, but not "that" much on the other side, even if Christ tells us to erase that line altogether. We're not willing to rub it out to join Christ if it means leaving behind relationships we find more valuable than the one we have with God.

My point is this: When preaching the Gospel "no matter what," find your own lines in the sand to follow the Gospel. Tap into your own fears of putting tradition, family, community, church, and friends at risk were you to change your view on the beliefs that bind you. Use this to empathize with your congregation. Empathize with their fears, their risks, and their limits, and recognize that each person will have different lines drawn on different issues. We can't know the wrestling of their hearts. We can't know what's at risk for them. Nor can we know the limits of Christ's compassion and mercy on all of us for our limits, because in Christ, compassion and mercy have no limits.

No matter what tone you feel called to structure into a tough message—whether it's hellfire and brimstone, raising-the-roof prophecy, or guiding people down the primrose path into an alien land of justice—breathe into it the compassion of Christ. Breathe into it the compassion of Christ whose compassion for us and the fears of all our listeners is why he went to the cross in the first place.

## Conclusion

We're called to preach the Gospel no matter what. Whether or not we or our listeners like what the Gospel says, we preach the Gospel as it is: Good News for all people. We know that to set aside our idols is our "get out of jail free card," and yet giving up our idols comes at a cost we may or may not be willing to pay. Egypt was bondage, but it was predictable bondage; it was the devil we knew. Wandering in the desert for an unknown length of time, without a map or exit strategy, toward a Promised Land we've only heard about but never seen only because someone else told us it would be worth it, is often not a lot to go on. Some days we wake up with more courage than others.

That's why we need to keep our gaze fixed on Jesus Christ who promises a love and peace greater than we can ask or imagine. By keeping our sights on Christ and Christ alone, we can exercise compassion with ourselves and others, and discern what truly needs to be said for their sakes. Nothing else matters as much.

# CHAPTER EIGHT

# Oratio for Sermons

### Good News

The more we embody the Good News, the less we can contain it.

### Prayer

I pray you proclaim clearly what you know of the Good News.

### Problem

We're afraid of what will result if we let loose God's glory.

### Vision

Our spirits magnify the Lord to the ends of the earth.

### Chapter in a Sentence

"Glory will out!"

### Latch

Finding a sermon message is effortless.

(The workbook to integrate this chapter with your backstory and preaching can be found at www.backstorypreaching.com.)

## Backstory

*"If [the disciples] were silent, the stones would shout out"*
*(Luke 19:40).*

Finding a sermon message is effortless. Does that sound naive? Simplistic? When it's no longer we who preach but Christ who preaches in us, Christ reveals the message already within us.

Thomas Keating wrote, "'Effort refers to the future and to what we do not yet have. Consent refers to the present moment and its content.'"[1] To rewrite this wisdom for preachers, "Effort refers to the sermon message we do not yet have. Consent refers to the present moment and the content of the sermon already within." We use effort to find a message when we view Scripture as a means to an end to produce a sermon. We use effort to find a message when we consider preaching as just part of the job, or a venue to expose our creativity, or when we sense the next sermon deadline and wonder how we're going to pull another one out of the hat.

But when we consent, we let God work on us in the present moment with the content of the text to reveal the message placed there. Other than to be present and witness, we expend no effort. *Lectio divina* works *on* us and *through* us to be present, to lead us to the sermon message as our destination, first for us, and then, for our listeners.

This third stage of *lectio divina*, *oratio*, then, is the expression that results from steeping in Scripture. After allowing the Word to work in us, the glory of God cannot be contained; glory will out. In the preacher's case, the glory that cannot be contained is the sermon. *Oratio* declares the Lord is effecting God's purposes, and we *know* so because in leading us to the message, Christ showed us a bit of the Promised Land. Through *lectio* and *meditatio*, and then *oratio*, Christ brings us to the sermon message, and for our part, effortlessly.

The direction of an effective sermon is guided by a one-sentence summary, which is discerned from the elements of Good News, Prayer, Problem, Vision, and, of all things, a Latch. Some of these elements show up verbally in the sermon, while others provide the backstory and are never spoken. These elements keep the sermon on

---

1. Maria Tasto, *The Transformative Power of Lectio Divina: How to Pray with Scripture* (New London, CT: Twenty-Third Publications, 2013), 38.

a straight and narrow path so Christ drives the listeners to the one and only destination of this sermon.

Here we turn to each element. In addition to the examples at the beginning of each chapter, I offer samples of these statements from several of my own sermons, and one complete sermon to show the statements put into practice.

## Preaching

*O sing to the* Lord *a new song;*
    *sing to the* Lord, *all the earth.*
*Sing to the* Lord, *bless his name;*
    *tell of his salvation from day to day (Ps 96:1-2).*

### The Good News

Good News separates an inspirational talk from a sermon. The definition of a sermon is that it must express Good News. Not necessarily in these words, but a sermon *must* declare that life is hopeful for the sole reason that Jesus Christ died for us and rose from the dead, making death irrelevant. If not, we render the "sermon" a speech. A sermon publicly declares that Jesus Christ is alive and here, right now, and we pray to God everyone listening will share our same faith.

Your statement of Good News summarizes your theology of Christ's saving work as a result of your *lectio divina.* When we engage the text prayerfully and are ourselves vulnerable and open to metanoia by the Holy Spirit, then we are changed. In the process of engaging the text as a response to God, God engages and transforms us because we come face-to-face with Good News. We become a little bit more a "word" of God. Christ wedges in a little more deeply and we are enlightened. We see. We know. We believe.

We want to tell people what we believe and proclaim the Good News that was revealed to us; that makes the sermon authentic and genuine. It tells our listeners that we, too, are on the same path, questing to recognize God right now and responding to God's hopes for us. To tell people what we believe makes us vulnerable because it publicly displays our love for Jesus Christ. This is what it means to be a witness to the living Gospel.

There may be multiple ways the Good News changed us in the encounter and multiple things we'd like to tell people. That's great! Make notes about it! But for any one sermon, *we only get to offer ONE piece of Good News.*

Even if the sermon is broken down into parts (like the traditional "three-point" sermon), there's still only one central story line. To be clear for listeners, the preacher has to identify it clearly and succinctly. Without a central story line, the sermon is likely to be unfocused, wandering, or "fuzzy." And the fuzzier it is, the less likely listeners will stay tuned in to what we're saying.

That being said, even the clearest Good News isn't necessarily what listeners hear, as demonstrated in chapter 7. We can't control what listeners perceive or the message they hear because the Spirit may need them to hear something else, or because fear may block the message. Just the same, to exercise the best practices of communication, clarity of thought is crucial.

It's necessary to clarify—by writing, dictating, or drawing—the Good News you intend to preach. We're often surprised to think we have the Good News clear in our heads, but when we're pushed to choose our words carefully and succinctly, we often discover our News isn't as clear as we thought. We may discover a run-on sentence with clauses or find that our theology is fuzzy. The Good News for a sermon needs to be unambiguous.

If you preach without notes or writing is difficult, state the Good News out loud as many times as necessary until you hear one complete sentence you can repeat without pause. An alternative is to draw the Good News as a comic strip. Regardless, that Good News statement acts like the beam from a lighthouse to guide us home. Its clarity helps ensure that *everything* in the sermon is said in service to the Good News we intend to proclaim.

What makes up our statement of Good News? The Good News is a public proclamation of "the astonishing thing" that Jesus Christ did and is doing *right now*. The goal is that anyone who hears the sermon will be able to say in one sentence, *"I heard Good News today and it is _____."* And "astonishing" doesn't necessarily mean "big." Indeed, the astonishing thing might be something very small that weighs only about five and a half pounds, has a bald head, and can be cradled in a manger. Big or small, subtle or earth-shattering, "astonishing" takes our breath away and we hope others will feel breathless by the revelation too. The Good News contains our theological backstory and declares who we see God is and what God is doing. What you believe about God's love, compassion, mercy, justice, and peace, and how God interacts with us will be made evident in your preaching. To articulate who God is and what God is doing helps you double-check yourself: Do I *truly* believe this? How do I know?

I began each chapter in this book with the six statements: Good News, Prayer, Problem, Vision, Message (Chapter in a Sentence), and Latch. I started each chapter this way not only to tell you what to expect, but also to model using them to select and organize aspects of faith for our sermons. In this post-Christendom era and new age of apologetics, it feels riskier, more vulnerable, and more necessary to declare our faith clearly and succinctly. Certainly globally, and more and more often locally, we lack a common culture of faith, so it's all the more important to be clear about what we believe and why. We who preach are ensconced in a love greater than all others. We strive to preach clearly so that others will strive to preach clearly with their lives.

The Good News statement is clearest when it's written as a complete sentence in the plainest language possible. There's a "Goldilocks" length that keeps the message simple but with enough direction to tell you exactly where you're headed. A statement that's too short might be too broad. For instance, "The Good News is, God heals" is true, but this message can go in a lot of directions. God heals bodies, nations, spirits, divisions, poverty, and grief. This Good News doesn't give enough direction to keep the sermon focused.

A clause is helpful, then. For example, "The Good News is, God heals *through* . . . ," so the focus is on the *means* by which the change is made. For example, "The Good News is, God heals through kind words." Or, if we append the clause "when" the focus is on the *effect* of the healing. "The Good News is, when God heals our blindness, we no longer look past those our city discards." Another example: "The Good News is, God heals divisions through the vulnerability of dialogue." That clause focuses on *what* is healed and *how*. Or, "The Good News is, God heals through those we least expect." This clause centers on both the means by which God heals and an aspect of God's character to choose surprising methods.

The opposite of the too-short and vague Good News statement is the too-long and unwieldy one. For example, "The Good News is, God heals the poor in spirit, the grieving, the lepers, the sinners, and the whole world." It would probably take a long time to unpack each one of those groups! Just remember, you'll get another chance to preach. We don't have to pack *all* the Good News in one sermon.

With so much Good News to choose from, deciding which piece of the Good News to offer is usually the hardest part of sermon prep. It certainly is for me! Because we can feel anxious to know what we're going to say, giving Christ the time needed to distill, sort, and cull the ideas takes a lot of trust. We need patience to let Christ set aside big, vague ideas for smaller, more focused ones. It's as if discernment requires us to watch him lift one Russian nesting doll out of another until only the one, smallest doll of an idea remains.

Discerning the Good News happens differently for different preachers. Some won't start writing the body of the sermon until they have their statement written. Some discover what they mean in the process of writing. It *doesn't matter* how or when you find it; the statement of Good News still acts as judge over what gets in and stays in the sermon. If you find the Good News in the process of writing, you still have to go back to edit. Check to be sure your stream of consciousness gets weeded out so there's nothing extraneous in your sermon.

Here are two examples from sermons of mine. For the story of Bartimaeus (Mark 10:46-52) I discerned, "The Good News is, Jesus is a respectful healer." And for the story of the "widow's mite" (Luke 21:1-4), "The Good News is, Jesus didn't save each one person; he saved everyone."

### The Prayer

We go first to be led to and transformed by the Good News ourselves. Now that we know how great that news is, we pray others will also be transformed. The statement of Good News describes the faith that emerged when we encountered Christ in Scripture. But since the Good News is not for ourselves alone but for all in need of that same saving grace, the Prayer states our hope that extends from us to our listeners.

The Prayer is why this Good News matters to anyone else. It's why everyone needs this Good News. It states what holy event will happen if people leave their quiet Sunday mornings at home to get to church on time to hear this particular sermon. In other words, it's the "So what?" What's so earth-shattering and heaven-building about this Good News that we pray in our heart of hearts for everyone to hear it? Though we can't control the outcome, we preach to put our listeners face-to-face with Christ and pray they follow him after the encounter.

The Prayer requires as much discernment, clarity of thought, and theology as the Good News. One informs the other, they work together, but the order in which they're discerned doesn't matter. You might discover the Prayer first and, through it, the Good News or vice versa.

Here are the Prayer statements I added to the Good News statements above: For Bartimaeus, "I pray you have the courage to ask for what most needs healing." Combine this with the Good News statement that Jesus is a respectful healer, and my sermon narrowed to focus on Jesus' character to wait on us, and the courage needed to face the changes healing can bring. And for the widow's mite, my Prayer statement was, "I pray you see that though not all were invited individually to follow Jesus, all are saved."

### The Problem

The problem is our human sin, our denial of the Good News, of trying to pretend the Gospel doesn't exist. This was explored in chapter 6.

The problem I saw in the story of Bartimaeus was, "The problem is we fear to be healed." And in the story of the Widow, I defined the problem as, "Jesus didn't fix each person's problems, so we might think he didn't fix everyone's 'Problem.'"

### The Vision

The Vision is the destination. It's an honest-to-goodness, flesh and blood picture of the Promised Land. If the Good News were really, truly, actually lived by the people who hear the sermon, what would they see? How would they be different?

The Vision is always incarnational. Because the Vision helps us see the potential, the promise, and the possibilities of the Good News, we see the world differently. When we see the world differently, we make decisions differently. That might mean we *do* something differently. We might do something in addition to, or instead of, what we're doing, or we might not do something at all anymore. The Vision might mean we *notice* things differently, and by itself, noticing might prompt us to take some action. In other words, the Vision is the congregation's *oratio*: Once they have encountered the living Christ, a reaction, an expression is called forth from them, even if that expression is an invisible, internal change of heart. It's the congregation's "So what? Why does this Good News matter to anyone other than ourselves?" The Vision is embodied and taken with them from the sanctuary because no one can contain God's glory.

My example for Bartimaeus: "All find the healing they need when they trust Christ." And for the Widow: "Any one person has limits to help, but as the whole Body of Christ, we have none."

### The Message

What are you trying to say? If a parishioner tells you she won't be in church but wonders what your sermon will be about, what will you tell her? If a parishioner were ill at home and his wife returns from church and tells him what was preached, what do you hope she'll say? *In. One. Sentence.*

The Message collects the Good News, Prayer, Problem, and Vision into one neat, summarized bundle. It declares in one sentence the point and meaning of the sermon. Sometimes the sermon ends with this sentence as a way to conclude. Other times it oversees as the backstory, never stated but always directing the action.

When discerning the message, answer this question out loud: "What are you trying to say?" Seriously. If you can't answer the question in one succinct sentence, it means you're not crystal clear what you mean. In that case, return to the text. Reread it several times. Look for either the puzzle you haven't quite solved (but thought you had) and explore that *meditatio* further, or the glint of gold that highlights Good News you hadn't noticed before. Repeat this process and take notes along the way of phrases you like, word choices, and the order. Keep repeating this process and rewriting your sentence until you can answer, "What am I trying to say?" without stumbling, adding clauses to clarify your message, and can say it the same way every time.

My message for the Bartimaeus story was, "Are you *sure* you want to be healed?" For the Widow it was, "Jesus showed he had limits to help one person, but as one Body, we have no such limits."

### The Latch

What will people *latch onto* as a way to understand the message? Will they latch onto a story? A parable? A proverb? A repeated phrase? What will hold the sermon together? What will be the thread that stitches together the six statements? What makes the whole thing stick together in a way that helps people remember it after they leave the sanctuary?

It's a balancing act to find the Latch that people hang onto without it taking center stage. A good advertisement is one that gets consumers to remember the product, not the jingle. I recall "Where's the beef?" was the advertising slogan for a hamburger chain, but don't remember the chain. "Oh, I wish I were an Oscar Mayer wiener" is almost impossible not to sing along with and, when you do, it's almost impossible not to notice the product contained in the jingle! We want people to remember the Good News; the Latch just helps it sink in, whether the Latch is a story, proverb, joke, or refrain.

The Latch I used for Bartimaeus was to retell the story from Bartimaeus's perspective. For the Widow, I told a story about a woman I know who appeared to many to be someone you could look right through as inconsequential.

### The Six Statements Together

Used together, the six statements function like a Supreme Court of judges who decide the final contents of the sermon. They keep the sermon going in one direction, toward the message, with a particular hope for its outcome: Good News for the world. This prevents the sermon from wandering aimlessly or thoughtlessly. As soon as we stray from that single destination, we confuse our listeners and their attention dissipates. This is extremely difficult to accomplish and requires a high-level skill of good writing. Since preachers are one of the few professional communicators who don't receive professional editing before we offer the fruits of our labors, we need all the help we can get. Hence, our demanding but beneficent "judges." My liturgics professor used to say, "Always know what you're doing during the liturgy and be able to justify your every action." Our sermon judges do the same job to push us to justify every word that leads toward the message. They make sure nothing gets into the sermon that doesn't bring us closer to that destination.

Even those who preach without notes and rely on the Holy Spirit in the moment need these judges. These preachers have to sort in real time which words are whispered by the Spirit and should be spoken, and which ones are not and shouldn't. Words zip to the tips of our tongues from our egos, memories, dreams, and random images. Some are inspiration and deserve to be aired, but most arrive from other sources and should remain tucked away. Our sermon judges help discern which words will lead toward clarity, and which will lead astray.

There's no rule whatsoever about which statement is discerned in which order, or whether you have one or all of them before you begin to write. The point is, they work as a team to offer clarity of message and a direction that both you, as the preacher, and the listeners can follow.

As I did for each chapter of this book, write (or dictate or draw) the statements as the first part of your sermon. Not because you'll say the statements out loud, but for your clarity and reference points. Once you've formed a final draft, proofread your manuscript or notes to decide whether every line, story, anecdote, paragraph, and word are *necessary and sufficient* to convey those statements. As you review each word, decide whether or not it is necessary:

If it's unnecessary, take it out.

If it's necessary but insufficient, expand it.

If it's necessary and sufficient, leave it alone.

### Hold the Listener's Attention

Once we have our sermon organized and know where we're headed, we still have to write the notes or a manuscript. There is a bonus section in the workbook (available at www.backstorypreaching.com) for tips on better writing for sermons, but here I cover what might be the most pressing need for preachers: how to hold the listener's attention. Here I'll offer two suggestions: "The Hero's Journey" and "Turn Scripture Upside Down."

*The Hero's Journey.* The "Hero's Journey" is the classic story pattern. The gist of the Hero's Journey is, the Hero starts off as one person, has a series of adventures, and ends as a different one.

If you're not familiar with the "Hero's Journey," follow along here with *The Wizard of Oz* to illustrate the pattern.

1. The Hero is introduced.
   *Dorothy Gale is introduced on her family farm.*

2. The Hero is presented with a problem.
   *Dorothy wants to grow up and leave home.*

3. The Hero tries to solve the problem.
   *Dorothy runs away from home. However, she rushes back when a tornado threatens her family. Upon entering her bedroom, she's hit on the head by a window, blacks out, and wakes up in Oz to find she has accidentally killed the Wicked Witch of the East. The Witch's sister, the Wicked Witch of the West, wants revenge. Dorothy must get past the evil sister through unknown lands to find her way to the Wonderful Wizard of Oz who, she is promised, will send her home. All Dorothy wants is to go home.*

4. The Hero tries one solution after another, but nothing works. Often there are characters who assist.
   *Dorothy receives help from the Scarecrow, the Tin Man, and the Cowardly Lion. The friends are disappointed when they finally reach the Wizard because he makes his assistance to Dorothy conditional.*

5. The Hero believes all is lost.
   *The Wizard's condition is the impossible task to kill the Wicked Witch of the West and bring back her broom as proof. After more dangers, the four friends confront the Witch in the Witch's Tower. The Witch lights her broom on fire and threatens the Scarecrow with it.*

6. The Hero (or the Hero's friend) stumbles upon a glimmer of hope.
   *The Scarecrow sees a bucket of water!*

7. The Hero (or friend) tries the new solution.
   *Splash! The water puts out the fire but also lands on the Witch, melting her.*

8. The problem is solved.
   *The friends bring the broom to the Wizard of Oz, who brings Dorothy home in the hot-air balloon.*

9. The Hero is changed as a result of the adventure.
   *"If I ever go looking for my heart's desire again, I won't look any further than my own back yard. Because if it isn't there, I never really lost it to begin with. . . . Oh, Auntie Em, there's no place like home!"*

We could apply the Hero's Journey to many of our own stories. Think of any trial you endured in which you learned lessons you couldn't have otherwise, and you, too, have followed the gist of the Hero's Journey. Jesus did too. In no way is this meant to trivialize Jesus, because the fact is, the life story of Jesus is still a true story.

Introduction: In the gospels of Matthew and Luke, Jesus is born, or in the gospels of Mark and John, is announced and arrives.

Problem: God's people are disconnected from God.

Attempted solutions: Jesus preaches, teaches, heals, does miracles, and says many shocking things to rile the authorities. He has help from the disciples. The solutions help, but don't solve the problem.

(Does Jesus ever believe all is lost? That's debatable, but perhaps he comes close when he vents his frustration, "How long must I be with you, you faithless generation?")

Glimmer of hope: Foreshadowing the Passion.

(Jesus is the reluctant Hero when he asks if the cup can be removed from him. He's asking, hoping, there's another way.)

All seems lost: Jesus dies.

Problem is solved: There's a shocking twist that only Jesus saw coming: resurrection!

The Hero is changed as a result of the adventure: Jesus is seen post-resurrection with his wounds, speaks, and gives final directions to the disciples.

Sometimes the Hero's Journey is spun out in individual stories, including short stories about Jesus. For example, Jesus enters the desert, endures the devil's temptations, and emerges prepared for ministry (Matt 4:1-11; Luke 4:1-14). A short-short story is when Jesus has his mind changed in the brief exchange with the Syro-Phoenician woman (Matt 15:21-28). Many biblical stories follow this story pattern. Consider the Israelites' escape from Egypt; Paul's conversion; the Good

Samaritan; and the story of the Samaritan woman at the well. There are many Hero's Journeys in the Bible, which is one reason the Bible still holds our attention, even when we know the stories' endings!

Translating the Hero's Journey to preaching, a sermon can recount the story of a biblical character who takes a journey, encounters God, and is changed. Who are they before, what do they endure, and who are they at the end?

Or, the congregation is the Hero. For instance, maybe the congregation doesn't want to give up comfy old "Egypt." "Egypt" might represent "the way we do things around here." Or "Egypt" might be the congregation's tacit agreement about *those people* who are excluded. Or maybe "Egypt" is the comfort to remain in familiar grief with a dwindling congregation who, understandably, refuses to see the writing on the wall. This last congregation might be the reluctant hero in many sermons who could be led over time to envision resurrection after the death of the congregation.

With the preacher as the trusted guide, the congregation is taken on the Hero's Journey in which the congregation is the hero, or the congregation is the vicarious hero as they see through the eyes of biblical or other contemporary characters. Through many "dangers, toils, and snares"[2] the congregation is changed and emerges into a better place, the vision of the "Promised Land."

*Turn Scripture Upside Down.* Even if a sermon doesn't tell a story per se, it can tell a story of exploration about a problem in the text when something doesn't make sense. This is especially interesting when we have always assumed a passage makes sense but, under closer scrutiny, it doesn't make any sense at all! As mentioned before, for example, why did Jesus ask what Bartimaeus wanted Jesus to do for him? It was obvious Bartimaeus was blind, so why didn't Jesus just heal him? Why ask him first? The other example I mentioned is that Eli's room isn't in the Temple. Why the Keystone Cops routine?

There are five elements to turn a Bible story upside down in a sermon. The first two elements could happen in either order. The important thing, however, is the conundrum isn't solved until the end. It's the mystery, the tension, that holds people's interest.

---

2. John Newton, "Amazing Grace," 1779.

1. Show the way the story has always "made sense."

   For instance, "Of course Jesus would heal someone who's blind like Bartimaeus!"

   Or, "Of course Samuel mistook Eli's voice!"

2. Show the "glitch."

   "If the need to heal blind Bartimaeus were so obvious, why did Jesus ask him, 'What do you want me to do for you?' Like, 'Duh!'"

   Or, "We assume it was an easy mistake for Samuel to think it was Eli calling. But where, *exactly*, was Eli?"

3. Build the tension by showing various solutions don't work or they complicate things further.

   "Why did Jesus ask Bartimaeus what he wanted? It might have been because of X, Y, or Z."

   Or, "Where was Eli? There's no sleeping chamber. So where could he be?" Then describe the Temple campus. In truth, Eli gets farther and farther away from Samuel making the likelihood that Samuel would mistake the voice more and more unlikely.

4. Resolve the tension.

   "Jesus asked Bartimaeus because to see again would turn Bartimaeus's life upside down, and not all for the good. Bartimaeus needed to choose for himself whether he *really* wanted this miracle."

   As for Samuel and Eli, "The 'Keystone Cops' routine maneuvers Samuel to get him disoriented, in the dark, and alone with God."

5. What does this new understanding of the story mean for us?

   "Accepting Christ's healing doesn't necessarily mean everything will be roses and sunshine, but Christ offers the healing we need when we're ready for it."

   Samuel shows us, "We often listen most closely to God when we're disoriented by life, we're in the dark about which way to turn, and we let ourselves be alone with God."

## Conclusion

The six statements result from organizing our experience of transformation by the Word through *lectio* and *meditatio*. Finding the sermon Message is effortless when we let Christ be the driver and take us to the sermon's destination: the Vision of God's promises. Once we have seen the Vision, we want to show others. The sermon itself is the *oratio*, the outward manifestation of this experience to be made more like Christ. The six statements guide the sermon to go in one direction and act as the judges to determine clarity of thought, message, and purpose.

We still need to write the sermon or organize our thoughts and offer a sermon that holds listeners' attention. Our listeners enter the worship service as one person, we escort them through the service—asking them to face their problems of sin and facilitating their encounter of Christ through Word, sacraments, and gathered community. They repent and leave a different person, more like Christ. Now that they know this "new" Good News for themselves, they won't be able to stand to keep God's glory in, and they, too, will bring that Vision to others.

*Oratio* ensures, "God's glory will out."

## A Guide to *Oratio*

1. Prepare yourself with your sermon prep plan.

2. In any order, answer the following:

   What do I believe is the Good News in this text? What's happened in real life to persuade me this is true?

   Why don't I/we believe the Good News? What's my/our problem? What's the "calf" I/we won't let go of?

   Because of the Good News, I pray I/they will see/believe/know/ take in _____.

   The Promised Land without dragging around that calf looks like _____.

   The one thing out of this sermon I want my listeners to hear is _____.

   The best way to get my point across will be _____.

3. Once these are complete, fill out the following and put them at the head of your manuscript or wherever you can refer to them easily for organizing sermon notes.

   I believe the Good News is (complete sentence): _____.

   I pray my listeners see _____.

Our Problem is _____.

The Vision is _____.

The Message is (complete sentence): _____.

The Latch is _____.

4. Organize your thoughts. Make sure the sermon has a beginning, a middle, and an end.

   Decide on the order for the components. Suggestions: write an outline; make a mind map; put major ideas on 3" x 5" cards and shuffle them until you like the order.

5. Write (or draw or make sermon notes).

   If the blank page intimidates you, freewrite for ten minutes on one of your statements. For example, think of a particular parishioner and write as if you were having a conversation, telling this person a story about how the Good News in this text impacts you or how you hope (Pray) it impacts them. Or weave a "What If?" picture when the Vision that God promised is realized, as in, "What if we lived a life of shalom now?"

6. *Contemplatio.*

   Once you've written a draft, give thanks and let it go for the day.

7. Revise.

   Revise your draft. Be able to justify that every word is necessary. Check it against the definition of an effective sermon: An effective sermon offers a clear message of Good News, authentic to the preacher, relevant to the listener, holding their attention, and inviting transformation.

8. *Contemplatio.*

   After the revision, give thanks and let it rest.

9. Tweak and practice.

   Look over the sermon one more time, mark your manuscript as needed, format it on your page or device so it's easy to read.

   If you don't use a manuscript, one suggestion is this: Have your opening line, each major transition, and last line memorized. This allows you to be relaxed because you know how you're starting and in a way that gets people's attention; you know where you're headed with each major transition so you don't wander too far afield in the moment; and you don't accidentally ramble at the end because you know when to stop.

Practice as many times as you need so you can be focused on your listeners rather than on your manuscript or notes.

### Sermon Statement Examples

*Year A, Proper 4*

Good News: It is not too wonderful for the Lord to soften our hearts so we can look each other in the eye.

Prayer: I pray you see we are not one another's enemies.

Problem: Arrogance that one's "side" is absolutely right; fear of change and loss of control.

Invitation to Transformation: *"Suscipe me."* ("Receive me.")

Message: Is receiving one another too wonderful for the Lord to accomplish?

Latch: The phrase, "Suscipe me."

*Year A, Lent 1*

Good News: The astonishing thing is, God makes us righteous through our tears of contrition.

Prayer: I pray you see that "The best wine is made from grapes watered by tears."

Problem: We conceal what will set us free.

Vision: We live released from the past when we accept the grace offered through the sorrow of our sins.

Message: We are made righteous by God through tears of contrition.

Latch: A story and the proverb I wrote above.

*Year C, Proper 12 (Colossians 2:6-15. Full sermon follows.)*

Good News: We are an Easter people of "stubborn gladness."[3]

Prayer: I pray you see the fearmongers for who they are and be glad in Christ.

Problem: We think we'll be safe when we revere those who spout fear.

---

3. Elizabeth Gilbert, *Big Magic: Creative Living Beyond Fear* (New York: Riverhead Books, 2015), loc. 79 of 2455, Kindle.

Vision: To live glad and fearless lives knowing we are safe in the
resurrection.
Message: We are an Easter people of stubborn gladness.
Latch: Repeated phrase, "Easter people of stubborn gladness."


In the epic, winner-take-all basketball game of the universe, it was
"Team Jesus" against "Team Everyone Else." The game was rigged
before it started, because on Team Jesus there was only one player.
Not surprisingly, at the end of the game it looked like the winner was
going to be Team Everyone Else. But . . . Team Jesus had the ball. Just
as the buzzer sounded and Everyone was rushing him, Jesus threw a
Hail Mary from the far end of the court. He swished it and won the
game of all time. There would be—no—rematches.

As a result of Jesus' miraculous win, the team rosters changed. It
was no longer Team Jesus against Team Everyone Else. It was just Team
Jesus—plus Everyone. Everyone who *wanted* to be on the team, that
is. No tryouts, not even prior knowledge of the game was required,
and short people were just as welcome as the tall ones. All you had to
do was say you wanted to be on the team, and you were on the team.

And so it was. Years went by. New people heard about the team
and signed up. Everyone was amazed that you didn't even have to
know how to dribble and you were just as much a part of the team
as everyone else.

On the side of the court, though, there were always some—*guys*—
leaning against the walls. Watching. And waiting. And sometimes,
when a player got tired and moved off the court for a breather, these
guys slid over close to the player. They would say something like,
"Good team, huh?" And the player would reply, "Yeah, the best!" And
the guy would then say something like, "Ya know, I've been watching
your moves. You're pretty good. But ya know, you're hookin' your
shots. I gotta way to fix that, if ya want." And the player would say
something back like, "Thanks anyway, but it doesn't really matter if
I make the shots or not. I'm just having fun on the team." And the
guy would say something back like, "Well, yeah. *Maybe.*" Then the
player would look at the guy with a kind of worried look and ask
something like, "What do you mean, 'maybe'?" And the guy would
answer something back like, "Well, nothin', really. I just mean, how
do ya *know* it don't matter if ya make the shots?" The player might
stop for a second, then say something a little uncertain, like, "Cuz

someone asked if I wanted to play. And when I asked what the teams were, they said there was only one team. I asked, then, how did anyone *win* a game? And they said that the game had *already* been won—so I figure . . . that means [voice trails off, uncertain] that it don't matter if I make any shots. Don't it?"

The guy would then kinda—freeze. Like he was in shock or some-thin'. Then he'd take a few quick breaths, real agitated like, and his face would get all red like he might explode. And then he'd drill the player with his eyes and say somethin' like, "Don't matter? Don't *matter*?! Look kid, you weren't there for the Big Game. I was. I *know* what happened. And let me tell you, it *matters* that you make the shots. You wanna make *sure* you're still on the team? Then you *gotta* make some shots. I'm tellin' ya, there ain't *no* guarantees in life, and you gotta show a little *hustle* out there."

Then, a few beads of sweat would pop out on the player's fore-head, and his eyes would get kinda big. He'd turn his head to look at the players on the court, then back at the guy. The guy would then sense the player's confusion. So the guy would then say somethin' like, "Look kid. You want my help, stick with me. You don't want it? Fine. Your funeral." And then the guy would slide over to another winded player and say, "Good game, huh?" The first player would take one more look at the players on the court, then hustle over to the guy's side. The guy would sense him, turn . . . and *grin*.

That, my friends, was the problem for the Colossians. There were some in the Colossians' community who couldn't believe that the game had been won for all time. They couldn't quite believe that Jesus was the crowned victor, that Jesus so completely annihilated his enemies that not only was Jesus' number retired, but so was any future competition.

Because it was so hard to believe, there were always *guys* on the sidelines looking to exploit their confusion. Always "philosophers" trying to lure disciples away with "empty deceits." They used the "elemental spirits of the universe" of fear and confusion, and a "se-cret knowledge" that only *they* could get the disciples on the roster of the winning team.

If Greek had had exclamation marks, bold, and italics, they would all have been used in this part of the letter. In fear for these dis-ciples, the letter writer cries out that Christ "disarmed the rulers and authorities and made a public example of them, triumphing over them." Meaning, "Don't be fools! Don't let them confuse you! Christ has already won! Don't join that team of liars who act as if they know something we don't, or who threaten you with their powers if you don't. Christ *mocked* their deceit in his *vulnerability* on the cross, and they have nothing but emptiness and chaos to offer you. We who are baptized are already on Jesus' team for life. Eternal life. What more could anyone offer you?" That's what the letter was crying out to the Colossians, and still is crying out to us today.

There are many who would delight to lure us away from Christ. There are many who use the elemental spirits of the universe like fear and confusion. Many who make promises of secret knowledge to keep us on the team. Many who give us messages that injustices cannot be righted, that violence is inevitable, that respect and dignity for all people is naive and impossible.

But theirs is the message of Good Friday when Jesus was dying and it looked as if all hope was lost. Theirs is the very message of hopelessness and empty deceit that Jesus mocked, defeated, and triumphed over while he hung on that cross. We are not a people of despair. We are an Easter people. We are an Easter people of stubborn gladness. "Stubborn gladness," a phrase coined by Elizabeth Gilbert, perfectly describes an Easter people's response to anyone who would lure us into a perpetual illusion that Good Friday is all there is.

As an Easter people, we are stubborn in our gladness that Jesus Christ triumphed over death and the grave and was resurrected. As an Easter people, we are stubborn in our gladness that Jesus Christ redeems everyone. As an Easter people, we are stubborn in our gladness that Jesus Christ is Lord of *all*. As an Easter people, we are stubborn in our gladness that no matter how powerful some are, the vulnerable power of Jesus Christ is the most powerful force in the universe. As an Easter people, we are stubborn in our gladness that the kingdom of God will one day be completed, because we know that God is just, and good, loving, and merciful, and one day, all things will be brought to rights by God and God alone. As an Easter people, we are stubborn in our gladness that with God's help, we will search for, and find, and take the steps to build that kingdom of hope, make that kingdom of justice, make that kingdom of peace that surpasses all understanding. As an Easter people, we are stubborn in our gladness and we show the world that Christ has triumphed simply *because* we are glad!

In fact, we are so stubborn in our gladness that we will happily confuse those who would lure us away with their compelling words of despair. We will happily *confuse* them by smiling at them *because* of our gladness and invite them to join us. In doing so, we are not so naive as to think the invitation will always go well. It won't. But we are an Easter people who make our song even as we go down to the grave, "Alleluia. Alleluia. Alleluia." As an Easter people, we are *that* stubbornly glad.

So, let's go cause a little confusion of our own. Let's smile at the "philosophers." *Because* we are glad, let's smile at those who try to lure us away with their empty deceits. Let's smile at them and ask them to join us, the Easter people of stubborn gladness.

# CHAPTER NINE

# Cultivate Wonder by Reading God

### *Good News*

The Good News is when we read God,
we are perpetually astonished and renewed by God's glory.

### *Prayer*

I pray you see wonder is essential
to preaching Good News week after week.

### *Problem*

We bore easily, even of the Good News.

### *Vision*

We are in awe of God at all times and all places.

### *Chapter in a Sentence*

When we read God we always preach from the overflow.

### *Latch*

A hymn and X-rays

(The workbook to integrate this chapter with your backstory and preaching
can be found at www.backstorypreaching.com.)

## Backstory

*Ever since the creation of the world his eternal power and divine nature, invisible though they are, have been understood and seen through the things he has made (Rom 1:20).*

Just about any new job starts off with novelty and excitement. We can hardly wait to get out of bed in the morning! We're intellectually stimulated, creatively engaged, and the challenges are so big and numerous we hope we can live up to them all. A while into the job, though, we usually learn we have the "chops" for it. The challenges feel smaller and fewer. The novelty wears off. What was once new and exciting becomes routine and ordinary.

This can be as true for preaching as it is for any other calling. We come out of our training excited and eager to preach, share the Word of God, and bring Good News to the world. But once we've been around the gospels a few times, the novelty wears off. We may not be so eager to see the Good Shepherd come 'round again. Or in the Revised Common Lectionary, the Transfiguration comes up twice a year, during Lent *and* on its own feast day in August. (What was the Lectionary Committee thinking?) Not to mention, how are we expected to bring good news of great joy to all the people *every* Christmas Eve? The story of that baby's birth hasn't changed a whit in two thousand years!

While preaching can become as tedious as any other calling, the potential consequences are worse. We can fail to see and share the Good News our people need to hear, whether it's their fifth Christmas Eve of life or their fiftieth. More so, we can fail to see the Good News *we* need to receive, whether it's our fifth Christmas Eve to preach or our fiftieth. The lack of discovery, the lack of novelty, and the lack of anticipation in that baby boy's story can cause us to lose heart as preachers, and our listeners can tell.

Fortunately, we're blessed to be in a vocation with innumerable assistants dedicated to preventing our ennui. We are surrounded by a great cloud of witnesses who perpetually point, showcase, shout, whisper, cajole, punctuate, and croon the glory of God! They must surely marvel that we could ever be bored for a moment, and wonder why we are not constantly lying prostrate in reverence.

You may have noticed I've used the expression "God's glory will out." That's a turn on the expression "Bad blood will out," meaning the unsavory character of a person will eventually be revealed. I don't know about that, but I do know absolutely that "God's glory will out." The glory of God cannot be contained, as Frederick Buechner explains: "Glory is to God what style is to an artist. The style of artists brings you as close to the sound of their voices, and the light in their eyes as it is possible to get this side of actually shaking hands with them. To the connoisseur, not just sunsets and starry nights, but dust storms, rain forests, garter snakes, the human face, are all unmistakably the work of a single hand. Glory is the outward manifestation of that hand in its handiwork just as holiness is the inward. To behold God's glory, to sense his style, is the closest you can get to him this side of Paradise."[1]

To behold God's glory—to sense, notice, and explore God's style—is to be on the path of perpetual divine discovery, resulting in the endless novelty of revelation and constant amazement. Indeed, to our five physical senses we can add and hone this sixth sense: the sense of God's glory. We hone that sense by cultivating wonder, the gentlest of questions; curiosity, the hunger to know God more; awe, the awareness that we are in the Presence of the ineffable; and gratitude, the bare-minimum and, sometimes, only response we are able to express. The more we refine our sixth sense of God's glory, the more it will build like fizzy joy under pressure that can't be held in, even in our fifty-fifth Christmas Eve sermon.

The great cloud of witnesses particularly relies on wonder, curiosity, awe, and gratitude to turn our attention to God. These feelings beckon us to see God anew, hear God afresh, and fill us with so much reverence for God that God's glory simply *must* be expressed. Glory will out.

### *Reading God*

O love of God, how strong and true,
Eternal and yet every new;
Uncomprehended and unbought,
Beyond all knowledge and all thought.

---

1. Frederick Buechner, *Wishful Thinking: A Seeker's ABC* (San Francisco: Harper, 1993), 35.

O wide embracing wondrous Love,
We read thee in the sky above,
We read thee in the earth below,
In seas that swell and streams that flow.

We read thee best in him who came
To bear for us the cross of shame,
Sent by the Father from on high,
Our life to live, our death to die.

We read thy power to bless and save
E'en in the darkness of the grave;
Still more in resurrection light
We read the fullness of thy might.
(Horatius Bonar, 1808–1889)

This hymn from the Episcopal hymnal[2] is one of my favorites. The hymn suggests we can *read* God. What does that mean? What of God is manifest that can be *read*, and what do we learn? The hymn encourages us to read God's actual, given self here:

Sky

Earth

Seas

Streams

In him who came

Darkness of the grave

Resurrection light

Of course, to read God is not an uncommon theme in Scripture. There is no place God is not contained, giving us the opportunity to read what spills over of God's presence. God is read in the image we find in one another's faces (Gen 1:27), in the heavens, angels, and mortals (Ps 8:3-5a), and day and night speak of God's glory (Ps

---

2. *The Church Hymnal*, 1982 (New York: Church Publishing, 1982), #455. Lyrics, public domain.

19:1-4). Shouts and hosannas filled the streets as people watched Jesus pass by on a donkey, and just in case the people fell silent, the stones under his feet were prepared to take over (Luke 19:38-40). All of creation, Paul writes to the Romans, has been reading the invisible God since the moment God bonded one atom to another (Rom 1:20).

Reading is a symbol system representing something beyond itself. Letters are patterned to form words, and words point to the things they represent. Words are then arranged in a particular order to create meaning by forming a sentence. But words and sentences aren't the only symbol systems we learn to read. We read numbers, music, and colors; human faces, clock faces, and the faces of the deep; electric waves, nebula arrays, and X-rays.

Our entire world is a symbol system for God. Everything God created points back to the One who made it. Plus, humans take the starting materials God made and shape them into something else. That's how we end up with books and songs, poetry and paint; buildings, cars, boogie boards and planes; EKGs, telescopes, and images of the body's veins. All are symbols that point to God's imagination working through our own, using the raw matter God invented. These symbols are the great cloud of witnesses. They point to God's glory where we read an infinite number of stories and come closer to their Creator. We read thee, God!

My husband is an interventional radiologist. When he was first learning to read X-ray films, he was bewildered when trying to discern one fuzzy gray blotch from another. One fuzzy gray blotch was a healthy organ, but another fuzzy gray blotch was a cancerous tumor. Or maybe the first fuzzy gray blotch was the tumor and the other one the healthy organ!

It took him years of practice to be able to read the blotches and sort healthy organs from cancerous tumors. Then, once he learned to read the blotches, his training wasn't done. He had to learn to tell a story about those blotches to his mentors and, of course, to the patient. Sometimes he had to tell a story about healthy organs, and sometimes he had to tell a story about tumors. Regardless, he had to tell a story about where the blotch was located, what kind it was, how it grew, what would happen to it without an intervention, and if an intervention were warranted, the result expected.

The story he told depended on the listener. To his mentors he had to tell the story in "medicalese." To the patient he had to tell the story as simply, understandably, and compassionately as possible. We could say in a sense, radiologists are niche storytellers. They tell stories of one particular genre. Moreover, the stories they tell are not original to them. They tell stories someone else wrote. Actually, someone "elses." Radiologists tell a story written in collaboration by God, the human body, radiology techs, and the imaging machine. Once they receive the story as a computer image, radiologists read and translate it and tell the story again, honing it for the listener.

Like radiologists, preachers are niche storytellers. We tell stories about God: God is our genre. Also like radiologists, we tell stories that are not original. We tell the stories God wrote (and continues to write) in sky and earth, seas and streams, in humanity and all God created. And most legibly, we read the story of God written in the One Who Came, Jesus. We learned to read the words of God's story in Scripture, and we can also learn to read God's story written everywhere in God's own holy and mysterious font, then practice telling that story in our own words, honing it for the listener.

How do we do this? Let me use my grandfather's engagement present to my grandmother I inherited to offer two stories about God I read there.

1. My grandfather didn't give my grandmother a diamond engagement ring. They were immigrants to the United States at the turn of the twentieth century and a diamond was beyond his means. Plus, he wanted to give her something more useful. Though they both earned little on the factory line in Detroit in the early days of General Motors, my grandfather saved enough money to buy his fiancée a beautiful gold pocket watch.

If I told you inside the back cover is inscribed "From Emil to Emilia, 1910," how old would you say the watch is? You could take the current year and subtract 1910, but that only scratches the surface. That watch is not just one hundred-plus years old. It's 4.5 *billion* years old, because gold is as old as Earth. Gold is made when two dead neutron stars collide.[3] The resulting violence creates microscopic gold dust.

---

3. "General Physics, University of California-Berkeley, "Astronomers strike cosmic gold, confirm origin of precious metals in neutron star mergers," October 16, 2017, https://phys.org/news/2017-10-astronomers-cosmic-gold-precious-metals.html.

That dust is gathered by passing meteors that crash into a forming planet, which makes the veins of gold. So, in fact, gold is even older than our planet. Talk about an antique!

Based on the age and violence required to make gold, I read this about God in my grandmother's pocket watch: "Long Ago and Far, Far Away, God Forged a Marriage in a Ghost-Star Fight." This story evokes awe in me. From star death, cosmic collision, and wandering gold dust, God made something beautiful, a sacramental relationship symbolized in the gold my grandmother carried every day of her adult life.

2. My grandmother's watch made me wonder about the origins of gold, then piqued my curiosity about gold's scriptural origins. It turns out gold is very prominent in our faith story. Here are three Bible trivia questions I wondered:

How many times is "gold" mentioned in the Bible?

What are the most-often mentioned precious metals and stones in the Bible?

What story in the Bible first mentions gold?

I don't want to spoil the surprise in case you get curious yourself. (To find the answers, look up the references to "gold" in a Bible concordance.) I'll only say, based on gold's prominence in Scripture, humanity has placed a very high value on gold since, literally, the beginning. This suggests God designed gold's properties to be placed on a sweet spot of the periodic table to make it uniquely functional and beautiful for us to use and enjoy. It's no wonder people give one another gold as a precious gift in wedding rings, episcopal rings, and pocket watches . . . and in our greed, what we'll do to get it.

The stories about the value humans have placed on gold and the resulting moral and ethical dilemmas include stories about the slaves forced to mine gold for Solomon's Temple; stories of exploitation during the boom and bust of the 1890s California Gold Rush; stories about forcing children in recent decades to mine gold; and the chemical mining now used to strip gold since most veins of gold are exhausted. Indeed, the cost to mine the gold in my grandmother's watch may be a higher one than I want to consider.

A second story line to result from reading God, then: "There's a Difference between Valuing God's Creation and Overvaluing It." What does that story line evoke in me? Disquiet. I feel a little squirmy inside wondering about the actual cost of my grandmother's pocket watch. Were I to know the total price paid—perhaps even by children!—to pull that gold out of a mine to be placed in the hands of a jeweler, then to form it artistically into my grandmother's watch, now to hang on a chain around my neck, I might have to weep with repentance. It makes me wonder about the ethics of the bliss of our ignorance to revel in much of God's creation without considering who paid what price for us to enjoy it. To read God, then, doesn't mean the story is always going to be pretty, comfortable, or to our liking. To read God leads us in every direction, from origins to aesthetics, from individuals to whole cultures, from delight to angst, from joy to sin, as well as from death to life.

To read God starts by wondering and getting curious to know more. It was wonder and curiosity that led me to notice and dig into that hymn. Wonder and curiosity also led me to ask questions about an ordinary object, my grandmother's pocket watch. The discoveries I made led to both disquiet and awe, and awe led to more questions, resulting in gratitude and excitement to have learned something new about creation and our use of it, our scriptural heritage, and God.

Wonder keeps our vision keen; curiosity, our minds engaged. The discoveries we make keep us in a perpetual state of awe, which shapes us constantly, creating a positive loop of gratitude and hunger to read God more. Boredom is banished beyond the edge of curiosity. The infinite witnesses who bear God's creative touch are in objects, people, and nature. There's nowhere we can go where we are not surrounded by God's witnesses, and each vies to get our attention. Each wants us to read its "book" about God, to ask questions, gape over the discoveries, and fall to our knees in gratitude. *Everything* you see at this moment—everything you touch, hear, and intuit—are signs and symbols that point to God. They point your sixth sense toward the Source, Wellspring, and Living Water of glory.

Now, it's your turn. I suggest you, too, read God so you can learn about and be awestruck by God all the time. Do this exercise now, or schedule a half hour for it on your calendar.

Prepare a timer for one minute, but don't start the timer until you finish reading the rest of the paragraph. Get as comfortable as you can. Take a few deep breaths so you feel relaxed but fully present and alert to your setting. When you start your timer, look around and take note of what you see. Perhaps you see books, a table, the chair you sit in. A ceiling. Your clothes. Your chest, as it rises and falls with your breathing. A window? Does it have curtains or a shade? What do you see outside? Buildings or trees? Clouds? The moon? (Start your timer now and look around. When the minute is up, continue reading.)

What caught your attention? What made you wonder? What piqued your curiosity? What odd thing made you remember its story about how it came to you? What made you wonder where it came from or how it was made? Go read God by digging into your questions in books on the internet, or calling someone who might know.

Now that you've tried this once (I hope), the fun part is to make this a practice. Make a journal for writing or drawing, create a digital file on your smartphone for dictation, and/or start an Instagram or Twitter feed. Or take a photo every day, like I do. Make it intentional. Commit to reading God in the witnesses who present themselves every day. Once you make a habit of reading God you won't be able to record them all, but you will have your own "curiosity shop" of witnesses to astonish you every time you look.

The bonus to creating your curiosity shop of glory is endless inspiration for sermons. You may not be able to choose which marvel to show your listeners next when *you're* the witness pointing to the glory of God.

## Preaching

*Take care and watch yourselves closely, so as neither to forget the things that your eyes have seen nor to let them slip from your mind all the days of your life; make them known to your children and your children's children—how you once stood before the* Lord *your God at Horeb (Deut 4:9-10a).*

If you've read this book in order and applied *lectio divina* to your sermon prep, I hope you've already experienced the impact that integrating a life filled with the spirituality of wonder, curiosity, awe, and gratitude can have on your preaching. *Lectio divina* is a spiritual and biblical process of divine surprise, creating an antidote to preaching ennui. When praying *lectio divina* for sermon prep, we discover the glory of God in the ordinary and extraordinary events, objects, and people in Scripture, and especially in "him who came." Each time we pray *lectio divina* we emerge altered, eager to go back and bring along our listeners on the same journey. Even when we are the reluctant disciple dragged into ethical dilemmas we'd rather not face, we still come through a little more liberated and want to live a little more justly, like Christ. When we take stock of who we were when we started, and who we are now that we've encountered Christ, we're amazed by God, what the Spirit can do, and the holy change we sense in ourselves.

Are you familiar with the expression "The devil is in the details"? Sr. Mary Luke Jones, OSB, taught me the opposite: "*God* is in the details!" She's so right! At the time she said this, we were preparing to host a party at her monastery. God was in the details as we arranged candles, tablecloths, dishes, flowers, and small gifts. We wanted it to be lovely. We wanted each guest to feel surprised by the beauty of the room and the obvious effort it required. Each detail witnessed to them that they mattered, that they were important, that they were worth our efforts. The details revealed our love for them and, therefore, God's love for them. God *was* in the details!

Similarly, God is in the details of Scripture. We can read volumes about God when we pay attention to the minutia. We often gloss over the details or consider them to be of little or no consequence. Consider, though, what I gleaned about God by reading into the details of gold. Two other instances when I wondered about details in Scripture led to delightful revelations about God and sermon messages. In one instance I wondered where Eli slept, and in the other I wondered where Jesus stood relative to the widow when she placed her coin in the Temple treasury box.

We can also read God in the details that *aren't* mentioned in the text; for example, what happened to the people after Jesus healed them? There was an honorable social safety net of sorts for the permanently ill or injured: begging. But what happened after Jesus healed them? There weren't any programs to teach them a trade, set them up in a hovel with a few chickens, and teach them to pay their bills. And if Jesus didn't invite them to join his band, they were left on their own. What do we read about God, then, when we dig into the details left unwritten?

To read God in the details, ask the fundamental questions of "who, what, where, when, why, and how?" For instance, *how* did people take care of themselves after they were healed? If there was no sleeping chamber in the Temple, *where* was Eli? On another subject altogether, but one we preach about every year—the crucifixion—consider these details: *Where* do the nails and beams come from for crucifixions? *Where* are they stored until they're needed? *Who* teaches the skills to wield mallet and nails to ankles and wrists? *How* do the executioners ensure the nails are placed correctly through the bones and into the beams to support the weight of the body? *How* is this training paid for? And very much related to this, *what*, exactly, does a tax collector, like Matthew, do?

By reading God in the details, we unearth God's imagination and the ways humans both abuse and glorify it. When we uncover these little mysteries, our spirits never run dry because we're always adding something new. Even when the details are grim, our spirits are fed because we learn in the smallest of ways how the light is not overcome by the darkness. We never have to feel like each sermon dips into a finite well of God's glory. When we read God in the details, the well overflows and we only have to dip our sermon cups into the spillover.

To put it another way, when we read God in *lectio divina*, our sermons come from the interest on God's generous endowment of ingenious creativity and grace, and never from the principle. We never get bored but are overflowing with anticipation to share the Good News we continually discover. As Micah Jackson says, "We don't have to *look* for something to say because we always *have* something to say."[4]

During your *lectio divina*, then, both personally and for sermon prep, slow down enough to see, hear, and touch the trivial and notice the absent. Awaken your sixth sense of glory by asking the "Five Ws and H" questions, and listen to what they say. The commonplace holds treasure troves of stories. Each one is a witness hoping you'll read them, because we read God in the details.

---

4. The Rev'd Micah Jackson, PhD, is the John Elbridge Hines Associate Professor of Preaching, Seminary of the Southwest, Austin, TX.

## Conclusion

Our entire lives, ministries, and preaching can be made up of perpetual surprises when we read God. Sure, ordinary tasks and the lectionary become routine, but that's not the same as getting bored, not when we read God in those tasks and cycles. The great cloud of witnesses point us constantly to God, knowing God's glory will out when we notice, wonder, get curious, discover, are filled with awe, and then, give thanks.

We never have to be bored, not with so many sacred wonders to be found. Every sermon prep session has the potential to fill us with the extraordinariness of God's presence, mercy, creativity, and grace. Every word in Scripture is fresh, and every moment we live consciously in God's presence reveals new, wonderful news waiting to be read and shared. With so much of God to read we can always be awestruck preachers, even if we are so blessed we preach our seventy-fifth Christmas Eve sermon.

# CHAPTER TEN

# The Preacher's Trust

### Good News

The Good News is
God trusts us with the Good News.

### Prayer

I pray you embody and hold sacred the trust placed in you as a preacher.

### Problem

We take this trust for granted.

### Vision

To live in awe and reverence of the trust placed in you as a preacher

### Chapter in a Sentence

Write your Trust between God, preachers, and your listeners,
and nurture it, always.

### Latch

The Trust

(The workbook to integrate this chapter with your backstory and preaching
can be found at www.backstorypreaching.com.)

### The Ten Commandments of the Preacher's Trust

*We gotta:*

1. Pray

2. Engage Scripture

3. Cultivate wonder, curiosity, awe, and gratitude

4. Seek respite in sermon prep

5. Trust you're loved no matter what

6. Craft effective sermons

7. Proclaim the Gospel, come what may

8. Preach ethically

9. Keep learning

10. Be accountable

The trust placed in us to preach is weighty, profound, and joyful and the coolest gig on the planet. We are charged to steward the Good News, to rely on the Spirit to rev the engine of the Gospel in the hearts of those who listen, and to start it in the hearts of those who don't. Indeed, as Tom Long wrote, "To be a preacher is to be entrusted with the task of speaking the one word that humanity most urgently and desperately needs to hear, the glad tidings of God's redemption through Jesus Christ." He continues:

> "You are my witnesses, says the Lord, and my servant whom I have chosen, so that you may know and believe me and understand that I am he" [Isa 43:10]. . . . The preacher as witness is not authoritative because of rank or power but rather because of what the preacher has seen and heard. . . . The preacher becomes a witness to what has been seen and heard through the Scripture, and the preacher's authority grows out of this seeing and hearing. . . . To call the preacher an authority does not mean that the preacher is wiser than others. What it does mean is that the preacher is the one whom the congregation sends on their behalf, week after week, to the Scripture. The church knows that its life depends upon hearing the truth of God's promise and claim through the Scripture, and

it has set the preacher apart for the crucial activity of going to the Scripture to listen for that truth. The authority of the preacher, then, is the authority of ordination, the authority of being identified by the faithful community as the one called to preach and the one who has been prayerfully set apart for this ministry, the authority that comes from being "sworn in" as a witness.[1]

Long packed so much into these two paragraphs I hardly know what to say about them. I feel as tongue-tied (or finger-bound) as I do when called upon to preach on a High Feast Day. What is there left to say? We could easily pray *lectio divina* with each of these phrases: "the one word humanity most urgently . . . needs to hear"; the preacher is authoritative *because* of what the preacher "has seen and heard"; the church's life *depends* "upon hearing the truth of God's promise"; and "it has set the preacher apart" for this "crucial activity." *Whoof!* (As in, big exhale here!)

In the weekly schedule of being sent to the Scriptures to discern a sermon, it's routine to take for granted the gravity of the task entrusted to us. Perhaps that's not all bad. If we didn't take our calling a little bit for granted, the magnitude and importance of preaching might weigh on us to the point our tongues would be heavy with fear. As preachers, we would find that particularly counterproductive.

On the other hand, when I was in college for my nursing degree, I had the chance to shadow an ICU nurse with fifteen years' experience. I asked her how many years she worked before she wasn't nervous anymore. She replied, "I'm always nervous. Not in the same way I felt in the beginning because I have experience now, but I'm always nervous. The lives of these people depend on me. If I don't have some butterflies, I'm taking their lives too casually."

A bit of holy fear is appropriate for preachers. We, too, can rely on experience, but a bit of holy fear lets us know we're not taking our call to preach too casually. Holy fear isn't the fear of failing, or ordinary nerves, or anxiety. Holy fear is knowing deeply that we're ordained by God and authorized by the church to be and bring the Word our

---

1. Tom Long, *The Witness of Preaching* (Louisville: Westminster John Knox Press, 2005), 13, 46–48.

listeners' lives and souls depend on. *Holy Toledo!* That's worth "bend-ing the knee" to Christ in awe each time we begin our sermon prep.

We need to have a healthy dose of holy fear also about the author-ity given to us. Ronald Heifetz defines authority as "conferred power to perform a service."[2] We are *granted* power by God, our church authorities, and our listeners to be a preacher of God's Word. They give us power in exchange for our service: in exchange for heading to the Scriptures each week and proclaiming the Word their lives and souls depend on. In offering us this power, listeners also offer to believe, or at least give us more than the benefit of the doubt, that what we say from the pulpit is true.

That power is the appropriate leverage we are given to offer the Gospel. We are neither to discount nor inflate this power. Indeed, this power requires our perpetually cultivated humility. Humility, meaning the truth as it is: neither higher nor lower, neither better nor worse, neither more nor less than it is, and neither more nor less valued than any other ministry of the church. We receive neither brownie points nor demerits from God for accepting the invitation to preach. Preaching is a ministry like every other we can put to Paul's "Many Gifts, One Body" test. If we puff a little hot air into our egos to believe preaching is more valued than God's call to teach, usher, mop the floor or change rolls of toilet paper, or show up for worship consistently when we're not *paid* to do so, then I respectfully suggest that's the time to head to confessors and spiritual directors.

The authority of the preacher is considerable, but the amount of trust people place in us causes the amount of authority we have to grow or shrink. The most powerful sermon in the world can't per-suade if listeners don't trust what we say is true. (The street preachers of my college days come to mind, especially Brother Jed. Powerful? Check. Loving? Hardly. So, trusted to offer the Word of God? Not a jot let alone a tittle.) Our whole lives proclaim the Gospel. People's trust in us is tested with every interaction. The more our lives match what we proclaim, the more trust people give us and the more authority we have. The more trust and authority we have, the more difficult

---

2. Ronald Heifetz, *Leadership Without Easy Answers* (Cambridge: Harvard University Press, 1994), loc. 692 of 4320, Kindle.

the message we can afford to proclaim and the farther our listeners will travel with us down rough Gospel roads.

Building trust takes longer than tearing it down, of course. The moment we say or do something that's perceived as "off" is the moment people might begin to wonder. They may brush it off or not recognize their own slight sense of dis-ease in the moment. Still, even a slight dis-ease is a distraction, just like bright orange shoes under the black robe of an acolyte. For instance, sometimes we goof with our sermon facts. (Like the time I was corrected after the third and final sermon of the morning. I said each time President Nixon had been impeached, but was finally reminded the president resigned before anyone could bring charges. Really, people? All three services before someone saved me from myself?) One goof is just a goof. But a second, a third, and a fourth start a pattern. The last thing we want is our listeners to question our facts because then, they might question the message. When they question the message, our sermons put curves in the road rather than making it straight for the coming of the Lord.

Before we even get the chance to offer facts (correct or otherwise) in our sermons, listeners trust us because we got vetted. Listeners trust the church structure that authorized us to preach, and they trust we learned from reliable authorities in our training programs. They also trust we've done our homework, that we studied Scripture, did our exegesis, and that the stories we tell are true. They trust we're offering them the actual Word of God that God wants them to hear. In short, they trust we're not making this stuff up.

If we were to ask listeners why they trust our sermons, most would include the items above. However, some will also note they trust us because the way they see us live is congruent with our words. They give us their trust because they have observed our integrity over time—meaning the way they see us live, move, and have our beings outside the pulpit is in keeping with what we say in the pulpit.

Moreover, I'm guessing they would say they trust us because they assume we have an ongoing relationship with God. They assume we pray and spend time reading God's Word. They assume what we say in the pulpit comes from God because we actually listen to what God has to say. Moreover, they assume we pray for them, our listeners. They assume there is a direct connection between what God whispered in our hearts and what they need to hear, exhibited by our choice of message, stories, and word selections. Unlike many assumptions, these are assumptions to affirm.

More than affirm, we can foster those assumptions and build trust. We can be faithful to our calling, confess our sins regularly, apologize and make amends for our mistakes, and be careful to act and preach with integrity. If so, we're doing everything we can to be worthy of people's trust. That's all any of us can do. It's another blessed limitation.

In sum, the trust, power, and authority people grant us as preachers is so essential to our ability to spread the Gospel and have it believed, it behooves us to spell it out. What do we as preachers promise? What's reasonable for people to expect of us? In what ways will we do our best to uphold the authority conferred upon us? What do we have to do to be found trust*worthy*?

I suggest we declare our commitment in a Preacher's Trust. This Trust is our pact with God and our listeners that outlines our side of the equation. This specifies what our listeners can expect from us as their preacher. A formal Preacher's Trust demonstrates our appreciation of the weight and joy of this vocation.

*Definition of the Preacher's Trust*

The Preacher's Trust

is the preacher's commitment

to abide in Christ

in order to be made worthy

of the authority granted

to preach the Good News.

For this Trust to be valid (real, genuine, and incarnational), and reliable (true every time), we preachers need to foster the divine triangle of trust between us, God, and our listeners at all times and places, not only in the pulpit. To build this Trust is to commit to the necessary and appropriate practices behind the scenes. Our backstory is to know that we, with God's help, are doing all we can to be worthy of, careful with, and filled with holy fear toward the power entrusted to us to preach God's Word.

The Preacher's Trust is like the Prayers of the People. There are ten required categories, but the language and choices for each are your own. Here I'll offer a brief explanation of each category, and if you read previous chapters none should come as a surprise. Indeed, they serve as a summary. The explanations are followed by suggestions for practice. The first five commandments of the Trust cover the backstory of our life and spirituality to "Be Good News," and the second five integrate them into our craft to "Preach Good News."

## Be Good News: Life and Spirituality

*We gotta.* Yup, we gotta. It's not negotiable. These are necessary for any preacher who desires to build and maintain the trust and authority placed in us.

### 1. Pray

Pray daily, early, often, and perpetually.

### 2. Engage Scripture

Read Scripture daily, early, often, and perpetually not only for sermon prep and to lead Bible studies, but first and foremost, because we are baptized.

Prayer and Scripture are essential because we can't preach about someone we don't know. If we don't know Christ, we can only talk about him in the third person. If we don't spend time alone with God and read Scripture for the sake of our souls, then sermons are only as good as repeating what we heard described thirdhand about a character in a movie. Not only does the integrity of our sermons depend on it, but our own lively, joyful spirits do too.

### 3. Cultivate Wonder, Curiosity, Awe, and Gratitude

"Wow! Look at what God did! Look at who God is!" Awe is to be caught up in something grander than ourselves, something ineffable that is more than our senses can take in. Awe is a cycle that makes us wonder who God is, which gets us curious enough to ask questions, which sends us on a quest to discover until granted an epiphany,

which fills us with awe and makes us sing God's praises in gratitude . . . which makes us start all over again. That's what keeps our
relationship with God alive no matter how many years we preach.
Without wonder, curiosity, awe, and gratitude, we preach *about* and
give a lecture. With them, we preach *from* an overflowing well of
*knowing* and offer a sermon of Fantastic News.

### 4. Seek Respite in Sermon Prep

We get to run away from all our other responsibilities. We get to
prepare a cup of tea or coffee, curl up in our favorite chair, turn off
all the noise and distractions, and be with God for a while. We get
to be led down trails to what we and our people need to hear. We
get to have revealed an aspect of the Good News that brings us to
our knees, and that we can't wait to share. Who else gets to do this?

### 5. Trust You're Loved No Matter What

We really are. God loves everyone, and none of us is the exception
to the rule. Thinking we are the exception is just another form of
pride. We're loved equally as much as everyone else. In fact, each of
us is perfectly average in the amount of love we receive in a sort of
original, divine, grade-inflation model: everyone gets an A+ in the
amount of love we earn from God, because all we have to do to get
it is be born. Congratulations!

## Preach Good News:
## Integrating Life and Spirituality with Our Craft

### 6. Craft Effective Sermons

We strive to craft effective sermons every time we preach with a clear
message of Good News that is authentic to the preacher, relevant to
the listeners, holding their attention and inviting transformation.

### 7. Proclaim the Gospel, Come What May

We may not face down lions in arenas anymore but we might face
down "lions" on social media, and on rare occasions, church graffiti,

threats, and church shootings. We're leaders of this faith, charged to preach Christ's Gospel as it is and not the Gospel we wish it were. Preaching requires discernment, courage, and support to step into the community of saints who have paid a price—large and small—for their faith. We preach the Gospel of unrelenting love, forgiveness, and mercy for *all* because we cannot contain God's glory, even when for some listeners that Good News feels like a threat.

### 8. Preach Ethically

To preach ethically is to preach authentically. When we preach from our deepest, truest selves, we have no need to steal someone else's words, or inflate or cherry-pick the facts. When we preach authentically, our preaching is faithful and, therefore, enough.

### 9. Keep Learning

Preaching is a creative art form offered in a voice only you can speak in your way. It's incumbent upon us always to search for and find the most effective means to help listeners hear the most important Word ever to be uttered.

### 10. Be Accountable

Contrary to all appearances as we're holed up in our offices writing our sermons alone, we're engaged in a communal event. We are one body of preachers offering Christ's voice to proclaim the Gospel, to make it real and known in the world. Preaching is hard, risky, vulnerable, and crucially important. We need each other for support and to hold one another accountable to the trust and authority given to us.

### Your Turn

Now it's time to take these categories and write them into your Trust. What, specifically, for a year will you commit to? You can make this a list, prose, poetry, stick figures, collage, or vision board. You can have one item in a category or fifteen, but don't skip any. Sign and date your Trust, specify when you plan to renew it, and note how you'll plan to remember the renewal date.

I hope you see that, although the Trust is another long to-do list, it's not a to-do list at all. *This is the integration of your life and spirituality with the craft of preaching.* There's probably nothing in the Trust that you wouldn't do anyway, because these are the things that matter most. Rather than adding to your day, this *is* your day. This is the baseline, your preaching raison d'être. It's the *other* things added to our to-do lists that make life crazy and out of control! *Not these.* These are the categories that make life God-centered, peaceful, creative, and joyful. These are the preacher's categories of incarnational faith.

Below are suggestions for each category, followed by my own Trust. It's important to be specific. Name names, describe the space, what time of day, how often, etc. The more concrete you make it, the more likely you are to practice it.

To reiterate, this isn't about keeping tic marks next to each "accomplishment." *This is your intention to* be *a trusted preacher, who speaks the Word of God as authentically as you can.* This is about who you are, your Backstory of Trust. Be prayerful as you discern with God, and perhaps with a spiritual director, how you are called to "Be Good News to Preach Good News."

## Suggestions

### 1. Pray

- Daily (which days of the week and at what time)
- Perpetual (e.g., Read God; Jesus Prayer; "Sacrament of the Present Moment"; manual labor; talk to God)
- Contemplative prayer
- Corporate (Morning Prayer or daily Eucharist)
- With family or friends, in person or online
- Retreats
- Journaling
- *Examen* of conscience
- Sacrament of reconciliation
- Walking labyrinths
- Fasting

## 2. Engage Scripture

- Pray the daily Office.
- Pray *lectio divina*.
- Follow a theme (word study; biblical genre; a character).
- Listen to audio Bibles or daily podcasts.
- Read Scripture with spiritual masters (e.g., Ignatian Bible Study).

## 3. Cultivate Wonder, Awe, Curiosity, and Gratitude

- Enjoy nature (get outside; examine objects; read books; watch DVDs; listen to or record nature sounds).
- Explore science (read books, magazines; watch YouTube; conduct experiments).
- Create and lose yourself in art.
- Read literature.
- Read and write poetry.
- Take photos and post daily on social media, or add to an art journal.
- Write in your journal.
- Buy flowers for your office desk regularly.

## 4. Seek Respite in Sermon Prep

- Prepare the physical space as carefully as liturgical space.
- Determine time of day.
- Create and follow a sermon prep ritual.
- Prepare yourself to slow down and enter sacred time and space.
- Pray.
- Breathe.
- Do yoga.
- Ask for what you need to give sermon prep your best self.
- Create a daily schedule for completion and keep that schedule as the highest priority.

### 5. Trust You're Loved No Matter What

*by God, Jesus, and the Holy Spirit*

- List names of those with whom your relationship doesn't depend on the quality of your preaching.
- Write and practice a mantra to repeat when surprised by an unkind response to your preaching.
- Have a list of those you can call for the postmortem when you're not happy about how a sermon went, i.e., your "tribe" who knows what it's like to be in the pulpit . . . and who will tell you the truth.
- Create a list of Bible characters and saints who also had to negotiate being lauded and vilified by the not-so-pleasant.
- Talk to a therapist.
- See a spiritual director.
- Consider the spiritual "giants" who "have your back." With whom might you hold imaginary conversations?

### 6. Craft Effective Sermons

- Conduct peer appraisals.
- Seek listeners' appraisals.
- Engage a preaching coach.
- Identify preaching skills you want to hone (which ones; how; for how long; with what support?).
- Listen to effective preachers (who? how often?).

### 7. Proclaim the Gospel No Matter What

- What/who will give you courage for a difficult sermon?
- Who in the congregation could you bounce ideas off of?
- Have a self-compassion plan.
- Have a list of colleagues who are willing to vet the sermon first.

### 8. Preach Ethically

- Preach as yourself and only yourself.

The Preacher's Trust   153

- Don't steal others' words.
- Don't alter numbers, Bible verses, or facts to suit your purposes.
- Trust that your preaching is enough.
- Invite dialogue and differing points of view.

## 9. Keep Learning

- Use online preaching resources.
- Read preaching books.
- Attend preaching festivals.
- Appraise your own sermons and others'.
- Participate in preaching mentorships.
- Listen to sermons online.

## 10. Be Accountable

- Spiritual director
- Therapist
- Preaching buddy
- Preaching coach
- Commit to review your Trust at a certain interval and share the revision.

### My Preacher's Trust

Reviewed every March 13 on the anniversary of my ordination to the priesthood.

In gratitude, awe, and humility for the trust held between God, my listeners, and me, this is my Preacher's Trust.

### Pray

Monday through Friday, I commit to my Morning Time from 6:30 to 9:00 to re-create my spirit. This time includes meditation, contemplative prayer, and sacred reading. I also pray daily for the preachers I serve in Backstory Preaching and for all preachers.

## Engage Scripture

During my Morning Time I commit to listen daily to an audio Bible podcast followed by *lectio divina* and journaling on a word, phrase, or question that arose from the podcast.

## Cultivate Wonder, Curiosity, Awe, and Gratitude

During my Morning Time I commit to Read God daily and take a photo when applicable. Weekly I commit to read books that inspire from nature, art, or spirituality. I also commit to set my intention to be with God when I exercise, play my instruments, and create art.

## Find Respite in Sermon Prep

I commit to follow my sermon prep ritual (brain dump, prayer, freewrite, and coffee). In addition, I will engage in *lectio* online with the Backstory Preaching community. *Meditatio* will be scheduled Tuesday and Wednesday mornings in my office with a candle burning. *Oratio* will be conducted Thursdays online with the Backstory Preaching community. I will write my sermons on Friday mornings and tweak on Saturdays in my office.

## Trust You're Loved No Matter What

This is the mantra I practice: "The relationships I hold most dear are not at stake." These particular relationships include God, my husband, and three friends. Knowing I'm loved, I'm free to speak the Gospel. I also commit to seeing a therapist periodically and spiritual director monthly.

## Craft Effective Sermons

I commit to do my best to stay faithful to the process; listen to skilled preachers online at least twice a month; read six books per year about writing and preaching; intentionally practice one skill each sermon; self-appraise my sermons using the definition of an "effective sermon"; and take part regularly in peer appraisal circles.

## Proclaim the Gospel No Matter What

I commit to pray for the courage to remember my fiduciary duty that the needs of my listeners come before my own. I commit to pray for the courage to sacrifice my comfort, reputation, or security if that's the result of preaching God's love for all people.

When there's a difficult text, I commit to the *lectio divina* process to accept the text as is. If there's a difficult message I feel called to preach, I commit to vetting it with at least two people in advance. I will have my mantra in my pocket along with the names of the people I hold most dear.

### Preach Ethically

I commit not to break the trust of my listeners by intentionally presenting others' work as my own. I will verbally cite sources, directly or indirectly and fully in manuscripts. I will recount true stories as accurately as possible and not alter them to suit my own purposes or evoke certain emotions. I commit to looking at more than "one view" during sermon prep especially regarding controversial subjects, and present differing opinions as appropriate. Finally, I pledge to preach a good enough sermon when needed.

### Keep Learning

I commit to read six books per year that assist with preaching (preaching; public speaking; good literature; poetry) and talk "all things preaching" with other preachers who are equally as passionate about our craft at conferences, meetings, and Backstory Preaching. I will attend at least one preaching conference per year.

### Be Accountable

It's programmed in my calendar to review my Trust annually every March 13th. I will share its revision with my spiritual director and my Backstory Preaching colleagues. I will also continue in my peer mentorship group, peer sermon appraisals and mutual prayer, and schedule a monthly Quiet Day the last Friday of every month. I will maintain a dedicated "Preacher's Trust Journal" in which I will record and track my Trust, and journal in it during my Morning Time.

By the grace of God, this is my Preacher's Trust.

The Rev'd Lisa Kraske Cressman
March 13, 2018

## Conclusion

I hope you pray about and write your own Preacher's Trust to honor and integrate your life and spirituality with your preaching craft. If you feel comfortable, include me in your accountability and send me a copy of your Trust at support@backstorypreaching.com. I would sincerely be honored to read it.

To be a preacher is hard, wonderful, risky, vulnerable, inspiring, sacred, and amazing. There's no end of learning and growing in the ways of God or the Gospel, so we are constantly surprised and amazed; boredom has no chance in our vocation!

I hope you find *lectio divina* a transformative process that makes you into the Word of God you preach, so that it is no longer you who preach but Christ who preaches in you. I also hope you will be excited to preach because you're awestruck by the Good News you *know*.

I pray you know you're loved and your message is enough. I pray your preaching is a prayerful response to God, and that you always have the courage to preach, come what may. I also pray you live in gratitude for the great cloud of witnesses who constantly point to the presence of God.

Thank you for accepting your call to preach. We need you to preach. *I* need you to preach. I need you to tell us your incarnation of the Gospel. No one can preach your way with your backstory other than you. Bring all your spirit, all your life, all your relationship with God into your sermon. Let the Spirit integrate it so you *are* the Good News you preach, because you, Christ, and the Good News are One. Then God's joy, and ours, will be complete.

*Deo Gratias. Amen.*

Yours faithfully,
Your fellow preacher,
*Lisa+*